PN Review 244

VOLUME 45   NUMBER 2   NOVEMB

SOME CONTRIBUTORS

Ange Mlinko is the author of five collections, most recently *Distant Mandate* (2017) and *Marvelous Things Overheard* (2013), published by FSG. She teaches poetry at the University of Florida. **Liz Lefroy** was winner of the 2016 Café Writers Prize and the 2011 Roy Fisher Prize. She has published three pamphlets, most recently *Mending The Ordinary*. **Lisa Kelly** is chair of *Magma Poetry*. Her debut collection *A Map Towards Fluency* is forthcoming from Carcanet, 2019. **Jee Leong Koh**'s *Steep Tea* (Carcanet) was named a Best Book of the Year by *Financial Times*. **Laura Scott** is one of the poets featured in Carcanet's *New Poetries VII* anthology. Her first collection will be published by Carcanet in 2019. **Marilyn Hacker** is the author of thirteen books of poems, including *A Stranger's Mirror* (Norton, 2015) and sixteen collections of poems translated from the French. She lives in Paris. **Nina Bogin** was born in the US and lives in France. Her fourth collection *Thousandfold* (Carcanet) will appear in January 2019.

Editorial

'PERHAPS ONLY BAD POETS become poets. The good ones, though they may wax vatic and oracular in public, and though they may even have full-fledged masterpieces behind them, know full well that they can never quite claim the name.'

Christian Wiman's new book *He Held Radical Light: The Art of Faith, the Faith of Art* (Farrar, Straus & Giroux) is brief and generically challenging. It combines anthology, memoir, meditation, theology, critical exploration, standing apart from the hectic fray of twitter assaults and batteries, blog and Facebook campaigns, all the shriller bat-calls that drive the distracted Muses deeper and deeper into the wilds. It listens in poetry for 'those moments of mysterious intrusion, that feeling of collusion with eternity'; the terms are theologically loaded and yet even readers resistant to theology may recognise what is meant here, those 'spots of time', perhaps, 'which with distinct pre-eminence retain / A renovating virtue' or, as Wordsworth preferred later, 'a vivifying virtue'. Or like Barthian 'flashes' that re-illumine and transfigure (even if only for a moment) the over-familiar.

Wiman, who for a decade edited *Poetry*, has written ten books of poems, a memoir and *Stolen Air: Selected Poems of Osip Mandelstam*. He is that rare creature, a professor of literature *and* religion at the Yale Institute of Sacred Music and Yale Divinity School. He knows that a holy mountain, whether Parnassus or not, survives though the public world has given itself over to the excitements of instant response: outrage, retro-outrage, correctness, incorrectness. It is possible to engage in considered dialogue with poems and poets, and with readers. They demand it, they deserve it. We deserve it:

> I stayed up late last night reading the letters of A.R. Ammons, who for years sowed and savored his loneliness in lonely Ithaca. 'Keep Ithaka always in your mind,' wrote Constantin Cavafy, 'Arriving there is what you're destined for.' And he did, Ammons, keep that mythical Ithaka in his mind, which is to say in his poems, decade after decade of diaristic ramblings that are as flavorless as old oatmeal this morning, as null and undifferentiated as deep space – then lit up suddenly by a meteoric masterpiece that must have surprised the workaday writer as much as it does the fatigued reader.

The meteor poem is 'The City Limits', which he quotes, and then remembers Ammons whom he met when he was an undergraduate. He evokes who he was himself three decades ago, and then who Ammons was. Wiman was attending one of his first poetry readings:

> [...] ten minutes into his reading he suddenly stopped and said, 'You can't possibly be enjoying this,' then left the podium and sat back down in the front row. No one knew what to do. Some people protested from the pews – we were in a place that had pews – that they were in fact enjoying it, though the voices lacked conviction and he didn't budge. Finally the chair of the English Department [...] cajoled the poor poet into

continuing. Ammons mumbled on for another fifteen minutes before the cold mortification of the modern poetry reading, and the beer-lacquered bafflement of press-ganged undergraduates, did him in. 'Enough,' he muttered finally, and thudded his colossal body down beside his wife like the death of faith itself.

*

The word 'Faith' in the book's title blinks like a warning light. That's what it's about, what Wiman is about: faith in a sense older and more challenging than we normally encounter it in the neighbourhood of modern poetry, and yet the sense of it nuanced, maybe even *modern* in what it has required of the writer, the poem, and of the reader willing to go along with him. Wiman wears his theology lightly enough so as not to offend those steeled against traditional faith. 'Nothing poisons truth so quickly as assurance that one has found it.' His meditations include alerting human anecdotes, the kind that change our sense of a writer and of writing. When the late Donald Hall eats a burger and declares:

> 'I was thirty-eight when I realized not a word I wrote was going to last,' I felt a galactic chill, as if my soul had chewed tinfoil. I was thirty-eight. It was the very inverse of a calling, an ex post facto feeling of innocence, death's echo. In a flash I knew it was true, for both of us (this is no doubt part of what he was telling me), and yet the shock was not in that fact but in the nearly fifty years of further writings Don had piled on top of that revelation.

One is struck by Hall's understanding of his place in the order of poetry, and by persisting in what he seemed to acknowledge as radical failure. Mary Oliver reads *The Faerie Queene* in order 'to spend what time I have left with masterpieces' – words that had lasted and might, despite the current age that forgets, politicises and misvalues, or revalues them, still last.

Wiman's book is about the rewards and also the perils of a calling that can never quite deliver the poet, or the reader, to its inferred, its intended destination. It is a kind of road novel, without a destination on the map, yet with an existential purpose. The human act of writing (he talks of his own practice, he is *in* his book, a subject), the body bending over page or keyboard, is in a living engagement with the language and literature that has shaped it, as with the world in time it occupies. Spots of time are in their expression shared, providing access, often indirectly, obliquely, slant. They are points of communion. 'Poetry itself – like life, like love, like any spiritual hunger – thrives on longings that can never be fulfilled, and dies when the poet thinks they have been. And what is true for the poem is true for the poet [...].'

Cover Story

Koen Vanmechelen, 'Evolution 1'

KOEN VANMECHELEN, artist and political activist, has confronted the issues that arise from humanity's relationships with other species, in a range of forms and media: painting, sculpture, photography, film, installation, performance. His subject matter is wide and various but he is best known for his insistence on the plight of the chicken, numerically the most abused animal on the planet. Exhibitions of his work are often tied to the establishment of community projects in which groups of local women are given the means to run their own free-range farms stocked with cross-bred chickens whose resilience, fertility and immunity to disease provide an instructive contrast to the fate of the average battery hen. The community projects are a practical demonstration of the care and respect owing to the species, while the artworks endow it with dignity – and even power. The image on the cover of this issue seems to conjure up a being from an earlier stage of evolution than our own: an indefinite creature that seems to hover between bird, dinosaur and mammal. It is the effect on the viewer that is definite: this is a creature it is difficult or impossible to imagine as under our control or at our disposal – the drawing is 4.9 metres x 3.2 metres.

Rod Mengham

Letter to the Editor

ANTHONY RUDOLF *writes* · In *PNR* 236 (2017), Grevel Lindop favourably reviewed *Exile and the Kingdom*, the most recent book of poems by Hilary Davies. So it was a surprise to read in the last *PNR* editorial that she had made an apparently excellent translation of the eponymous book by Albert Camus. This is a clearly a benign mistake on the part of the editor and, by the law of unintended consequences, may encourage admirers of Camus and Davies (and any newcomers) to reread (or read) both of these books.

News & Notes

Menard Press · *Marking the fiftieth anniversary of the founding of Menard Press, Anthony Rudolf wrote to us on 15 September:*

Menard Press (then *The* Menard Press) started life in 1968. Its first publication appeared in January 1969: this was the Michael Hamburger issue of the *Journals of Pierre Menard*, set on a typewriter and mimeographed in Oxford by Peter Hoy, co-editor of the magazine. For me, Jon Silkin was the exemplary poet-editor, Donald Davie the exemplary poet-critic and Michael Hamburger the exemplary poet-translator. Poetry translation was at the heart of our enterprise, but in addition to literary titles we published a series of pamphlets on the nuclear issue, one of which sold more than 14,000 copies, *Towards the Nuclear Holocaust* by Sir Martin Ryle, one of our Nobel Prize winners. The press became dormant in 2009, forty years on, having brought out about 160 books. Since then I have been pleased to publish two essays by the late Nigel Foxell, the fugitive poems of Caroline West and the press's first and last comic book, *Nightmare Scenarios*, dealing with mental health issues, by the poet and illustrator Matt Barrell, whom I first met in 1965, when he was a few weeks old. I am pleased to say that Shearsman Press has published a few reprints of Menard titles over recent years, including Jonathan Griffin's translation of Pessoa's *Message*. A short history of Menard and its origins in the exceptional era of the late 1960s can be found in the press's fortieth anniversary catalogue. Something was in the air, symbolised by Jenny Lee as the first Minister for the Arts. If you send me ten pounds, I will send you the catalogue and a Menard book post free. The press had its moments but a one-man band demands energies I no longer possess, and these days I have other priorities.

I end with a revised extract from my book *Silent Conversations*:

Vasko Popa's magnificent *Collected Poems* (published by Peter Jay at Anvil Press, now Carcanet) is prefaced by a poem, dated 5 June 1981, which Popa wrote overnight at the Cambridge Poetry Festival (founded by Richard Berengarten in 1975) on learning of the death of his main translator, that modest yet scholarly and authoritative Oxford philologist, Anne Pennington, who had an ear for his music. The next day Peter Jay, Daniel Weissbort and I sat at a café table and produced the following version together, which was first published as a *MenCard* and then in *TLS* before coming to rest in *Collected Poems*:

ANNE PENNINGTON
Until her last breath
she enlarges
her Oxford house

built in Slavonic
vowels and consonants

She polishes the corner-stones
until their Anglo-Saxon shine
begins to sing

Her death is like a short breath-stop
Under the distant lime trees of her friends

My fondness for this poem, my nostalgia for the circumstances of its creation, my pleasure in the translation by three friends, probably with help from Popa in French, all feed a dream of fellowship in or through poetry. Perhaps that was what Menard was about.

Publicity costs · In the *CB editions* newsletter, received on 29 September, Charles Boyle wrote tellingly about prizes and prize culture, after Will Eaves, a contributor to these pages, was shortlisted for the Goldsmith's Prize for his novel *MurMur*). Boyle reported himself pleased: 'Pleased, despite the reductionism of lit prizes, which take their form from what is increasingly (and depressingly) the only show in town, capitalist competition, winner takes all. But we work from where we are, which is not where we used to be (say, a century ago, when so-so poetry collections sold in their thousands and writers were paid many thousands of £££ by magazines for a single short story). Reading being no longer central to the culture, publishers are a little desperate for publicity for their books, to get them known to more than friends and family, and the prize culture has become embedded.

'Some prizes are more equal than others. There was a twitter flurry this week following the announcement that the Women's Fiction Prize (sponsored by Deloitte, Baileys and NatWest) had decided to charge publishers "a small fee of £1,000 for the sixteen longlisted entries, in addition to the existing fee of £5,000 – which remains unchanged – for each of the six novels shortlisted". The Costa Book Awards charge publishers £5,000 for each book chosen as a category winner (as well as requiring at least fifty free copies), plus another £6,000 for the overall winner. The Dylan Thomas Prize and the Man Booker Prize also charge publishers of shortlisted books several thousand £££ for non-transparent reasons such as "contributions towards publicity costs". (For comparison, total set-up cost for CBe in 2007: just over £2,000.) A number of the smaller presses are thereby excluded from these prize competitions (and even if they did enter books that were shortlisted, would lose money, because sales income would not meet costs).'

'Hijab-wearing mermaids' · Book banning in Kuwait has hit the news. The issues for the Kuwaity authorities are political and physiological. Michelangelo's *David* cannot be displayed because of his genitals, Disney's *Little Mermaid* because of her pneumatics. 'There are no hijab-wearing mermaids,' said Shamayel al-Sharikh, a Kuwaiti women's activist. If Disney wants to sell mermaids in Kuwait, there may soon be some. 4,390 books have been banned since 2014, 700 in the last eleven months, and to our knowledge none has been unbanned despite protests. The committee of censors numbers twelve. Sometimes reasons are given, sometimes mystery surrounds the decisions. Maya Angelou, Gabriel Garcia Marquez, Naguib Mahfouz and George Orwell are among the proscribed authors. A new branch of bookselling is evolving, the banned bookdealer. Kuwait allows public protests, hence the welcome focus on this issue. The Kuwait Book Fair is the third largest in the Arab world, a further irony. 'There is no book banning in Kuwait,' the Ministry of Information declared: 'There is a book censorship committee that reviews all books.' And an assistant minister proclaimed, 'In Kuwait, over the past five years only 4,300 books were banned out of 208,000 books – that means only 2 percent are banned and 98 percent are approved.'

Poetry prizes · The Poetry Foundation in Chicago announced this year's winners of its major awards. The Ruth Lilly and Dorothy Sargent Rosenberg Poetry Fellowships were awarded to Safia Elhillo, Hieu Minh Nguyen, sam sax, Natalie Scenters-Zapico and Paul Tran. The $25,800 fellowship is among the most generous awards available for young poets in the United States. 'Our 2018 fellows created their own trails and important beautiful markers for those who will follow them into the future,' Don Share, editor of *Poetry*, said.

Rafael Cadenas · The Queen Sofia Award for Latin American poetry has been given this year to the Venezuelan poet Rafael Cadenas. Poet and essayist, now in his late eighties, he is a prolific writer whose books first appeared in 1946 (*Cantos iniciales*) and who has received major awards in Venezuela and in Latin America more generally.

Matthew Sweeney · *Peter Pegnall sent us this appreciation, written in August:* NEVER BELOW PAR, Matthew Sweeney was a master hypochondriac; he would seize on any hint of malaise and be spellbound. This extended to his friends' ailments and treatment, he would leave not a detail unprobed or unnamed. This was not through misanthropy or negativity: it was his love of life and of friends and partners that compelled him towards the anguish of loss, the geography of pain. That he should fall victim to Motor Neurone disease, following the awful demise of his beloved sister from the same sickness is a dreadful irony. Reality more than outstripped imagination and I am not at all surprised that he displayed character, tenacity and courage in adversity. Like the White Queen in Alice, he had already expressed his pain before the worst occurred.

He spent childhood in Donegal, beautiful, bleak and desolate. Ballyliffin, his hometown, is a place where nothing happens, not twice, as in Beckett, but 365 days every year. The Beckett link is telling, Matthew wrote dark fables laced with gallows humour, never explaining or apologising, but searing his way into the reader's memory. His children's poetry has something of the same grim fascination, he knew the story of growing up too well to condescend or sentimentalise. His readings of his own work were dramatic and uncompromising, he could snarl and tease, set puzzles without solutions. He was as driven by the art of Tom Waits as he was by more literary models, was never stuffy or pusillanimous, wore a black leather jacket with sinister panache.

As a friend, his smile was a blessing, his delight in fine food and drink Jonsonian, his irascibility almost a public spectacle. Especially fond of lacing into editors and administrators, it is not surprising he never became an establishment figure, thank the good lord. He taught with real gusto and his candour was always creative rather than proscriptive; the list of poets assisted by his judgment and example is wide and will grow. I trust that, somewhere this side of the undiscovered country, he senses this.

Another neglected aspect of his work are two great anthologies, *Emergency Kit* and *Beyond Bedlam*, the first with Jo Shapcott, the second with Ken Smith, two of the very best. One covers the wild and playful and overtly or covertly political in contemporary poetry, often drawing on European and American writers scarcely mentioned in these narrowing shores; the other reaches back into history to chart the treacherous waters of mental health and creativity. A pioneer without imperial ambitions, Matthew had the ability to be a professional golfer. He would have graced the fairway and improved the fashions in sweaters and trousers. Better a poet, perhaps.

Publisher to Beckett, Miller & Selby · John Calder, an outspoken foe of censorship and always a controversial figure in the publishing world, died in August at the age of ninety-one. His Calder list, acquired and maintained now by Alma Books, published Russian classics, Beckett's poems, plays, novels and essays (his main claim to fame), Henry Miller and Hubert Selby's *Last Exit to Brooklyn*, prosecuted for obscenity in the Old Bailey in a case lasting two years. Calder was convicted, won an appeal, and that was the last major case of prosecution of a literary work for obscenity. Calder was also a bookseller, one of whose ventures was closed owing a number of small presses what were to them considerable sums and endangering a sector he had seemed to champion. His autobiography, *The Uncensored Memoirs of John Calder*, was self-published in 2001.

Blood from a stone · The Canadian poet, memorist, fiction writer, playwright and editor Priscila Uppal has died at the age of forty-three. She was suffering from synovial sarcoma, a rare form of cancer. She was born in Ottawa, her family originating in south Asia, and she was a Professor of Humanities and English at York University in Toronto. Of her eleven books of poems, *Ontological Necessities* (2006) was a finalist for the Griffin Poetry Prize. She was shortlisted for other awards as well, for her memoirs and other writing. In a very short time – just over a decade – she became known throughout Canada and abroad. Her first collection remains among the most memorable, *How to Draw Blood from a Stone*, published when she was twenty-three. 'Another Dysfunctional Cancer Poem', a late poem, part of an editorial project of that title she undertook with Meaghan Strimas, begins:

> My body and I have now entered that phase
> of relationship where all the quirks and ticks
> that used to tug at your heart are sources
> of irritation and argument. The monotony of being
> with you, day in and day out, going through the motions.
> We are now that couple no one wants to
> see in public, whose shopping bags hang like broken
> promises.

In 2013 she gave a series of readings with Tishani Doshi around Britain and Ireland, delighting audiences at events in Newcastle, Galway, Grasmere, Edinburgh, Liverpool and Sheffield. Her first UK poetry selection was *Successful Tragedies: Poems 1998–2010* (Bloodaxe). Her most recent book is *Sabotage* (Bloodaxe).

Friend of the Beats · In August the poet, editor, sportswriter and biographer Tom Clark died at the age of seventy-seven in a traffic accident in Berkeley, California. His books include *Light & Shade: New and Selected Poems* (Coffee House, 2006) and *Threnody* (effing press, 2006). He was a friend of the Beats, travelled with Ginsberg (later falling out with him), gave readings with Gregory Corso and with Robert Graves, and wrote the life of his mentor Charles Olson. His essays were widely published in Britain and the United States, and he edited poetry for the *Paris Review* during a crucial decade, from 1963.

A neighbourhood poet · Anthony Rudolf remembered his friend the poet and translator, musician and broadcaster Keith Bosley, who died at the age of eighty, in *The Fortnightly Review*, noting among other things, his skills as a non-professional musician. 'Before dinner at his house with Keith and family, some visitors would be invited to St Laurence's next door, to listen to him practising the organ for Sunday: a kind of aperitif. Bosley was [...] good enough not only to play the organ in public from the age of sixteen but also to accompany on the piano his first wife Helen Sava and his second wife Satu Salo, professional singer and harpist respectively.' He was a leading translator from the Finnish. But in his own right, 'He was a neighbourhood poet in the best and broadest sense of the word. The Chilterns, Berkshire and Buckinghamshire feature prominently in his writing.'

'A sort of mystical experience' · Boletines, the eighth Carlos Montemayor Languages of America poetry festival (which occurs every two years) was celebrated in October at the Nezahualcoyotl Hall in Mexico City, bringing together poets representing many of the indigenous languages of the continent from Mexico itself, with its enormous range of languages and dialects, Guatemala, Colombia, Chile, Canada, Brazil, the United States and elsewhere. The festival provides 'a privileged space for languages that usually don't enjoy so much exposure'. Natalia Toledo, the Zapotec poet from Juchitan, Oaxaca, declared it an honour 'to listen to other cultures, the first of the continent, which offer us their poetry, radical and beautiful'. She was one of seven hosts for the festival, organised by the Program of Cultural Diversity and Intercultural Studies (PUIC) of the National Autonomous University of Mexico (UNAM). It takes its name from the anthropologist, historian and writer Carlos Montemayor, who coordinated the festival until his death in 2010. 'Every festival, we have brought to the Nezahualcoyotl Hall a sort of mystical experience, for two or three hours, with an audience consisting largely of students, who are changed after hearing the poetry in different languages,' said Jose del Val, PUIC director. The festival also included talks and discussions between the poets, students and the public. This year the poets reading included Humberto Ak'abal (Mayan Quiche), Natalio Hernandez (Nahuatl), Elicura Chihuailaf (Mapuche), Margaret Randall (English), Briceida Cuevas Cob (Mayan), Ignacio Vieira de Melo (Portuguese), Louise Dupre (French), Fredy Chicangana (Quechua), Juana Peñate Montejo (Ch'ol) and Zara Monroy (Seri). The great historian, philosopher and translator Miguel León-Portilla was an honorary guest at the event.

Speaking with Stones

A Day in Leeds City Art Gallery

Vahni Capildeo

Hard food for hard folk. In Yorkshire we're so tough, we eat stones. Out in the heathland, the artist Anthony Earnshaw (1924–2001) 'made a wonderful find: a stone, or rather a half stone', which looked exactly like half a brown bread cob, lightly toasted, a working breakfast for a 'smash-and-grab raider'. When on display, it sits like a farmer's market escapee alongside a knife on the bread board which the artist's partner had been using in the kitchen. Is the most granitic county in England the most surreal?

This misleading bap is one of several satisfying items in the exhibition *Rock, Pebble, Quarry: The Sculptural Lives of Stone*, running until spring 2019 at Leeds Art Gallery's Henry Moore Sculpture Galleries. Our species has adapted to make sense by stones: place, boundary and memory are mentioned in the catalogue description. Still, the main thrust is the materiality of stone. You could read aloud the catalogue entry syllable by syllable, like placing cool pebbles in your mouth to release saliva on a long, hot walk: 'marble, red marble, basalt, black porphyry, alabaster, Hornton stone, Ancaster stone, Portland stone, limestone, slate, verde di Prato and serpentine'. Considered closely, stone establishes a quiet primacy; 'other sculptural substances' are included for their ability to 'impersonate' stone.

Do stones live? If we could speak with the ghost of Paul Nash (1889–1946), he might confirm that they are hyper-alive. Nash 'flushed a covey of wild stones' and 'found a stone nest'. The imprint of its 'Only Egg' gives a name to his photograph of flint and shale. Nash's 'The Circle of the Monoliths' is his response to Avebury's stones 'in their wild state', before their restoration. Their siskin reds and tanager blues are poised with performance-ready alertness on a skin of puddled earth.

Jon Wood (Henry Moore Institute), Nigel Walsh (Leeds Art Gallery), the poet Ian Duhig and I had met to discuss the possibility of organising a Stone Day of talks and performances, including opportunities to view the *Rock, Pebble, Quarry* exhibition. This happened on 11 July. As anyone will know, whether or not they have learnt to skim stones successfully, ground spices in a traditional mortar, defended themselves against wild animals or better-armed opponents, lifted a Neolithic hand axe by chance from the Water of Leith, or shiveringly noticed the cobalt blocks of dressed masonry stolen from some bloody, concealed, tumbledown slave-owner house and repurposed for a shed wall on a forested mountainside overlooking Port of Spain, something tingles in stone that has been worked, or that lets itself be used. There is mutuality. Jon Wood spoke of 'incision and decision'. He made stone seem softer, a thing of textures and effects, bringing in matters of light, phrasing and painting.

As a poet listening in to different kinds of expert, I experienced a freeing of the concept of stone from hardened or limiting literary associations, re-rooted into a refreshed field of words. The first session, 'Rock', saw Thalia Allington-Wood chairing Ian Duhig on 'Stones on the Tongue' and Andrew Moore on 'The Fascination of Stone'. To give a glimpse of the range and unexpectedness which every speaker brought throughout the programme, here are some brief details of how the stone conversations started off. Andrew Moore identified six stone themes: landscape; travel and exploration; metamorphosis; studying the rock face; prayer and meditation; and memory, myth and meaning. Moore shifted how we might classify substances, saying for example that cut glass was known in ancient Egypt as 'the stone which flows'. Although we were in a windowless lecture theatre, aware of the stones waiting to be viewed in the adjacent gallery, Ian, like a wizard, took us swooping through the city in which we were located: Leeds, whose buildings can clean up beautifully, having been planned as a place of multi-coloured stone. He reminded us that stone travels, and read a poem about a devil sandwich, which resonated nicely with Earnshaw's 'HA HA', quoted on the label for the bread-stone found object.

These introductory talks stand out in my memory not only for scholarly insights into the particularity of North of England surrealism, magic, freemasonry, and artists' responses creating a historical record of our relation to the geological environment, but also for their acts of reimagination. The language around stone altered its stoniness; stone became present to us as abject, changeable, a companion in our mayfly lives whose endurance is beyond our grasp. Stone was hailed as a common denominator, an embodiment of ideas, central to our perception of ourselves.

A screening of Sophie Bullen's film 'Quality, Value, Convenience' (2018) was the preamble to 'Pebble', where Nigel Walsh presided over Jeremy Noel-Tod's talk, '"Foolishly Admired": the Pebble as Poetic Object', and Will Atkins on 'Earnshaw's Prank Pebble: Some Notes on Deception and Failure'. The fiend's invention that is social media tempted me to live-Tweet Noel-Tod's thrilling series of carefully excavated quotations and shining analyses. One corner of Atkin's compendious discussion that caught my poetic mind was how photography interrelates with stone, creating angles and interpretations.

Bethany Maltby's 35mm shots of Huddersfield Quarry and Delabole Quarry were shown during the tea break, leading into the last discussion, by Jon Wood, Donna Roberts ('"An Indivisible Heritage": Roger Caillois' Eco-Phenomenology of Stones'), Hannah Sofaer ('The Interrelationship of Art and Place') and Peter Fillingham. Like Jeremy Noel-Tod, Donna Roberts cited André Breton; but rather than yield to the fancy of quasi-osmotic exchange between humans and stones, she seemed to posit an opposition between flesh and rock. I wondered why. Conferences can be productive of creative distraction; over the years, I have seen more than one would-be minute-taker poet moved to sketching pictures or drafting. In line with my peers' known waywardness, I took my pencil and wrote in capital letters 'THIRST & POROSITY'. Surely we and the stones had a lot in common.

At last we went out to join the artworks themselves, for 'Petrichor'. This is a recently invented word, which blends the Greek for 'stone' and for 'the blood of gods'. We need it to describe the smell of oncoming rain, or rather the effect of moisture on dry stone or earth, which releases oils. As I write about stone north of the Humber river, petrichor from untimely, climate-confused Antillean thundershowers is heavy in the air. The rain reacting with the sculptures in this case consisted of poetry (introduced by Nigel Walsh), from Michael McKimm, Jeremy Noel-Tod and me. Petrichor is two things at once and so is the memory of poetry. I am just above the Equator and the junction of two tectonic plates, in a bungalow where the garden walls and walkways have cracked into puzzle-pieces, damaged by a recent earthquake. I am also in the Leeds gallery, neighboured by Barbara Hepworth's 'Hieroglyph' of stone carved to let through twists of space, and by Peter Randall-Page's 'Red Fruit', a smooth-tooled, beefy pineapple that fooled a fly into settling on and investigating it. The reader becomes flesh and stone.

Letter from Singapore and New York

Jee Leong Koh

The barricades around Hong Lim Park were supposed to protect us against the possibility of anti-gay terrorism. We should even have concrete blocks in front of the barricades, the police advised, to stop any vehicular attack. What was left unsaid was that the barricades were first instituted a year ago to prevent any 'foreigners' from participating in Pink Dot, Singapore's annual gay equality rally. Citizens and Permanent Residents had to produce their identification papers at the one sole entry point to the park. Local politics for locals only, is the mantra of the People's Action Party (PAP), who has governed Singapore since independence from the UK. And so the political controls continue under the paternalistic guise of security and self-governance.

Like many others, I was outraged when the barricades went up in 2017. As one rally banner protested memorably, 'Out of the closet and into a cage.' I cast around for something I could do to express my sense of indignation about the wrongness of the situation. By that time, I had been awakened from political slumber by two key events.

First, the re-election of the PAP in 2015, with seventy percent of the popular vote, a reversal of a decade of decline in electoral support. Many political observers ascribed the unexpected result to a wave of gratitude and nostalgia after the death of Singapore's first Prime Minister Lee Kuan Yew. Whatever was the cause, the result was crushing for civil society. The hope for greater political freedoms and stronger democratic guarantees dimmed. The PAP would see the electoral victory as a mandate for their authoritarian style of government, and so they did. Grants were withdrawn from books seen as critical of the government. A documentary film about political exiles stayed banned from public screening.

Second, another shock hard on the heels of the first, the election of Donald Trump in 2016 as the POTUS. This result was followed, however, not by unhappy acquiescence, but by a tide of nation-wide protests. The Women's March. The March Against the Immigration Ban. The March Against Gun Violence. Living in New York City, I was in the middle of a great revival of popular action, which recalled for many people the mass civic movements of the 1960s and '70s.

It was not immediately clear what I could do on my annual month-long visit to Singapore. Public demonstrations are only legal in Hong Lim Park, and then only with a permit. Outside of the 0.94-hectare space, a single person protesting against the state can be, and was, prosecuted under a new public order law as an illegal assembly. Such restrictive laws, including detention without trial, are a lasting legacy of British colonialism; the Singapore government has merely expanded and updated them. Given the difficult situation, the ideal action, I decided, should take place outside the 'cage' but it should also avoid proscription as illegal. A double escape.

In addition to the state, I had to consider my relationship to local gay activists and, more generally, the local civil rights landscape. The organisers of the Pink Dot rally faced strong criticism from more radical quarters for accepting the barricades, but it was hard to see what else they could do beyond cancelling the rally in protest and wallowing in a moment of righteous anger. Patience was the better part of valour, and the organisers accepted the barricades in order to continue to grow the movement, which has increased tenfold in attendance in the ten years of its existence. In my own small way, I wanted to supplement, not contradict, what these intrepid activists have been building.

Pink Dot is easily the largest and most visible civil rights movement in Singapore, introducing many Singaporeans, gay and straight, to the idea and practice of public action. When participants wear pink and travel by bus and train to Hong Lim Park, when they make new friends and renew old ties during the picnic and concert, and at the climax of the event when they light up their pink flashlights to form the 'dot', which has grown more and more like the shape of the island of Singapore as attendance swells, Singaporeans are learning to stand up publicly for what they believe in and to call on the government to do what is right. The manacles of fear are being broken.

The fear reached even New York where in 2014 I started the biennial Singapore Literature Festival and the monthly Second Saturdays Reading Series, to bring Singaporean and American authors and audiences together for readings and conversations. Completely reliant on private donations for funding, I was worried that an overly explicit emphasis on human rights would alienate Singaporean donors. When I brought together these activities, including the Singapore Poetry blog (SP blog), under the banner of a new literary non-profit called Singapore Unbound – with the tagline 'Freedom of Expression. Equal Rights for All.' – I kept the support for gay equality understated.

The barricades changed all that. As Frost knew, good fences do not make good neighbours. They keep out, they keep in, they divide. Much as the proposed wall along the border with Mexico is a symbol of American xenophobia and racism, the police barricades around

Hong Lim Park is a symbol of Singaporean neo-colonialism. Like past colonial masters, the Singapore state treats its citizens as its wards and not as its sovereign.

The idea came to me out of nowhere. I would print five tank tops with the words 'Gay But Not Yet Equal' on the front and 'Equality for All' on the back, and wear them about every day while I was in Singapore. I would make visible my sexual orientation and the injustice against LGBTQ people. To increase the visibility, I took photographs with the friends I met and, with their permission, posted the images on social media. The gesture would have remained relatively unknown still, if an incident did not bring it to the attention of the national press. Some patrons, probably as few as two, of the gym that I frequented complained to the manager that I was illicitly conducting political advocacy on a 'nationally sensitive issue'. I wrote a Facebook post about this homophobic complaint and it soon became news. In the event, the gym decided that I had not broken any rule and allowed me to continue to wear my 'gay' tank top. On subsequent visits to Singapore, I gave away free tank tops to anyone who would wear them and post a picture of himself or herself online.

Gay but not yet equal. The words point out present wrong but they also point to future hope. Worn close to the skin, they feel deeply personal. Worn around town, appearing at the top of an escalator or at the bottom of a drink, they look matter-of-factly political. The question about the relationship between poetry and politics has been bothering me for some time now. Isn't poetry written in service to current political concerns merely topical, ephemeral or, worse, propagandistic? Isn't politics conducted through writing poetry impotent? More and more I'm persuaded, however, that although poetry and politics belong to two different countries, it is wrong, if not impossible, to build a wall or erect a barricade between them. For the benefit of both, they must have free intercourse.

The First Time

Visiting Donald Hall

LUCY CHESELDINE

In the poem 'Her Long Illness', printed intermittently throughout his collection *Without*, Donald Hall wrote vividly on his wife Jane Kenyon's terminal cancer:

> They flew all day across
> the country to the hospital for hard cases.
>   The night before Jane
> entered isolation in Seattle for chemo,
>   TBI, and a stranger's
> bone marrow – for life or death – they slept
>   together, as they understood,
> maybe for the last time. His body
>   curved into Jane's,
> his knees tucked into the back of her knees;
>   he pressed her warm soft thighs,
> back, waist, and rump, making the spoons
>   and the spoons clattered
> with a sound like the end man's bones.

As I landed in Boston, these lines clattered around my fuzzy head, ringing all too close to the bone. The comfort of limbs and bodies dissolve to cartilage; movement is end-stopped by modern transport and medical quarantine. My legs ached form the six-hour flight, as I stuffed them into a waiting car heading, now, to Donald Hall's calling hours at the funeral parlour. Don, as he became known to me over our correspondence, had been generous and forthcoming about his work and life. I was to interview him at his home in New Hampshire for my doctoral thesis. Until three days ago, I had been preparing for this conversation, but I suddenly faced a more muted dialogue between his words and our lives. At the kind invitation of his assistant, like the poet-couple, I too was on a disembodying pilgrimage from one box to another; at the destination, I would meet Don for the first time as he lay in his casket.

Don was not afraid of death. He stared at it form a young age, with humour, in elegy, and through a lifelong obsession with memory, making a symphony of these in his poems. Knowing this gave me strength during the two-hour drive to the funeral home. Upon arrival, in two small rooms, extended family milled around, sitting or standing: all giving the open-coffin a wide birth. In the first room, above a firm-looking sofa, hung a typical pastoral painting. A few horses milled around in front of a wooden barn, to the background of a grey sky. The scene summoned Elizabeth Bishop's poem 'Large Bad Picture'. Like her uncle's scene of ships in sunset, the horses were illusive: 'Apparently they have reached their destination. / It would be hard to say what brought them there, / commerce or contemplation.'

The uncertainty here is both palpable and charming. Is this the destination or have we further to go? As Don writes to Jane in *Without*: 'you know now / whether the soul survives death. / Or you don't.' It wasn't so hard to say what brought Don here in his eighty-ninth year, of which both commerce and contemplation were essential parts. His freelance life on Eagle Pond farm had been upheld by a ceaselessly reflective mind. And part of his capacity for longevity was owing, like the title of Bishop's poem, to an ear for a good joke. In one of my favourite anecdotes from *Essays Over Eighty*, he recalls a poet friend giving a reading in New England 'for a crowd of two': 'Gamely, she did a full reading from the podium, and afterward descended to shake the hands of her crowd. One was dead.' I told this story to my own small audience of Don's daughter-in-law and grandchildren as I stood lost for words and stunned by the sight of my first dead body. Thankfully, they too could see the comic side of darkness.

The funeral was held at South Danbury Baptist Church where Don and Jane were both once deacons. The minister would reveal Don's ongoing joke about his essay in *Playboy*, poet-friends would remember his extensive revision process and encouragement to young poets over bourbon. A retired pastor would call Don a 'prophet', and a sequence would be read from Ecclesiastics 3. Then the pews would all fall silent as we listened to a recording of Don reading 'Old Roses' and 'The Names of Horses'. Tears would fall and voices would begin again. I write these recollections as modal impressions because there was nothing finite about that day. His poems are threads still woven tightly into the New England community, and poetic history, into the time he spent editing the *Harvard Advocate*, numerous pamphlets at Oxford, and the interviews he carried out for *The Paris Review*. His impression is left, strung like a web, and because it already accounts for death, it accounts for continuity: distinction of the past is prom-ise of the future. Don was dressed for burial in a tie-dye peace t-shirt, a black dinner jacket and a large gold-black ring. His skin was bluish. In a way this felt right; he was Thomas Hardy's original air blue gown, or his own grandmother, Kate, in his poem 'The Flies', dying in her blue nightdress. He had absorbed the years of clarity and liminality, the contradictions and images of a life lived in poetry – a life making words shake and shiver in tandem with breath. The words came first, then the breath, but when the breath has stopped we still have the words.

The Customed Thews

Christopher Middleton's cottage

JOHN CLEGG

Christopher Middleton spent the August of 1958 just outside the small Cambridgeshire village of Bourn, in a cottage rented from friends of his parents. He was thirty-two, and had more or less disowned his first two collec-tions from Fortune Press (the earliest published when he was just sixteen). His ability was finally beginning to match his ambition; of the poems that would feature in the book he would come to see as his genuine debut, *Torse 3* (1962), 'At Porthcothan', 'Oystercatchers', 'Waterloo Bridge' and 'A Bunch of Grapes' had all been composed around that year. But these poems, although they were certainly his best so far, lacked the invocatory strangeness which had attracted him to poetry in the first place. He was at risk of becoming a Movement poet.

The poem he wrote during that holiday, 'Male Torso', turned him onto a different path. Visiting his parents in Cambridge, he'd read a poem in the *Times Literary Sup-plement* by Rosamund Stanhope – an incredibly under-rated writer, incidentally, who will feature in a subsequent column – entitled 'Miniature Snowstorm'. Stanhope's poem would be the major influence on Middleton's; to her vision of childhood encompassed in a snowglobe, he counterposed a vision of adulthood encompassed in artefacts he'd seen in Munich's Staatliche Antikensam-mlungen: the male torso of the title and the black-figure Dionysus Cup. Other motifs he borrowed freely from the limited sources he had to hand: the 'bleating queen' and 'needle oars' are taken from Tenniel's illustrations to *Alice Through the Looking Glass*, which I suspect Middleton was reading to his eldest daughter at the time; the 'small horned worms' of the final stanza are from Dante; ele-ments of the fifth stanza are taken from *Paradise Lost* (book four); he was rereading both poets as part of an (abandoned) research project on mythological mountain ranges.

Visiting Bourn sheds not much light on the poem, although the room where Middleton wrote (on the first floor, I think the window in the photograph) looked out on some chickens, which may have suggested 'hutch of mud' in the penultimate stanza. Both cottage and village have undergone substantial additions since 1958. (The old manor house has been split into two properties, so there's some lucky soul whose address is '2, The Manor, Bourn'.) It's a bit of a mystery what Middleton got up to out there, with two small children (a three-year-old and a not-quite one-year-old); if you find yourself stuck there today, the best thing to do is walk to Kingston nearby and look at the astonishing fifteenth-century wall paintings in the parish church, but that can hardly have kept the toddlers entertained for a month. It's a pleasant three-hour walk from Cambridge, down the Wimpole Way, and if you go on a weekday you probably don't have to book to get a seat in the gastropub. I went on a weekend and had lunch instead in the marvellous Indian restaurant on Alms Hill, where I was the only customer. 'Male Torso' is one of the few early pieces that Middleton reprinted every chance he got; it occurs in every selection he made of his work, and when the *Chicago Review* interviewed him in 2005 for a Middleton special issue, it was one of the few poems he mentioned by name.

from The Notebooks of Arcangelo Riffis

MARIUS KOCIEJOWSKI

Some months after Arcangelo died, I passed the house where he'd lived on Earls Court Road. It was my first time back there. A single sheet of metal was hammered over the front entrance, as if to say there could be no admis-sion to this place other than via death's portal. Somehow this struck me as appropriate – the blocked entrance, the stairs beyond it going not *up* anymore but *down*, down to Hades, so very Roman I could just about smell the burning frankincense. Why was he so iffy when I said Mother Church snorted pagan fumes? Why did every-thing Christian have to be *year one*? It's a common error for humanity to think itself at the beginning of time. It makes for messy consequences. Anyway the building was up for sale, voided of its occupants, and I tried to picture the empty room at the back of the top floor where, from 1.00 to 3.30 precisely, we spent our Sunday afternoons, the purple flock wallpaper falling away in sagging folds, the smell of damp and cigarettes, the ceiling yellowed with decades of smoke and in places browned from rain leakages, the dust rising from the armchair each time I sat down a little too hard on it, the window which on blustery days shook in its rotting embrasure, the wasps that got in from somewhere and stung my friend who, close to immobile, could not escape them in time, and the rubbish that he'd allowed to accumulate because he saw value in it, if not for now then later, because who knew what purpose it might serve.

It was always so dim. A single 40-watt lightbulb sheathed with dust hung from the middle of the ceiling, which he hardly ever turned on because it was the same lightbulb that was there when he moved in and so he got it into his superstitious head that it should not blow as long as he lived there. 'Switch it off,' he cried when one time I was trying to find something for him amid the clutter of his room. 'Damn it, switch it off.' I flicked it on and off several times not because I'm sadistic but because I've never known anyone who could play so hard on my nerves. Only later I began to understand he measured against that lightbulb his own existence. Which filament would blow first, its or his? The bedside lamp barely lit the space between ourselves. We addressed each other through a nicotine haze.

When I looked through his window I could see, diagonally opposite, the window of the room where, some decades before, my girlfriend and I lived for a couple of years. A spool of fishing line would be sufficient in length to join the two places. It was yonder, in that room, in October 1974, I first met him. It was there we ate. Spaghetti, yes, damn it all, I should have read the signs immediately. What I might have been spared otherwise. My girlfriend worked as receptionist at a small hotel in Nevern Square, close to Earls Court Road, from whence she brought home tales of a night porter, a strange American who detested America, who recited poetry, wrote it, and who, upon hearing of mine, wanted to meet me. She brought him home, a cougar on a leash, a caged look in his eyes. We invited him to stay to dinner and no sooner did the boiled water go down the plughole than came the first signs of tension between us. We had only the most minimal cooking facilities, a single gas flame, but we adapted as young people do. We first made the sauce, then boiled the spaghetti, and, when the latter was done, warmed up the sauce a little, quickly before the other went lukewarm, tipped the spaghetti onto the plates and topped it with the sauce. It was at this critical juncture that we were treated to the first of Arcangelo's many harangues. 'One should always,' he said, 'mix the spaghetti and the sauce *prior* to serving. No self-respecting Italian would ever put the sauce *over* the pasta and never, absolutely never, should a spoon be allowed for its consumption.' Admittedly he was right or at least partially so because there are exceptions to the rule, but rightness can be wrongness in certain situations, especially with respect to manners, which, after all, were invented not in order to subvert or disguise truth but in order to allow for reasonably smooth running between people and, besides, I was never one to put up with another man's hectoring tone.

London, August 25, 1969. Winter is here, tra la. They've bitched Woburn Square – the rotten scuttlers. Give the sons of bitches time, they'll raze the Tower of London & there build a Wimpy house. Look what they've done to St Paul's – an Orwellian fantasy. In its surroundings it looks as out of place as the Prophet Isaiah at a table of transatlantic Rotarians. It has become a truism in Britain that whatever happens in the USA is sure to follow over here within five years. And so it does – Colonel Saunders & the McDonalds feederies are elbowing into folk memory the pubs and fish n' chips parlours. One has only to sit tight & watch the rot drift across the Atlantic & catch the air here. Remember Ezra Pound's lines in 'Canto LXXX' in *The Pisan Cantos?*

and the Serpentine will look just the same
and the gulls be as neat on the pond
and the sunken garden unchanged
and God knows what else is left of our London,
my London, your London [.]

Letter from Wales

SAM ADAMS

I have been providing some marginal assistance to a research project on Frank Lloyd Wright and, as often happens in such cases, have had my curiosity aroused by the subject. 'Lloyd' may be sufficiently common in the anglophone world for its Welsh roots to pass unrecognised, but the word is an adaptation of the Welsh '*llwyd*', meaning 'grey'. The '*ll*' is a single letter in the twenty-eight letter Welsh alphabet and its sound is formally described as a voiceless alveolar lateral fricative. The aspirate in the anglicised spelling of the name of the sixteenth-century physician and antiquary Humphrey Lhuyd is an attempt at an approximation to the Welsh pronunciation. 'Lloyd' is not an unusual companion to 'Jones' in Welsh names. Richard Lloyd Jones, Frank's maternal grandfather, borrowed it from his mother Margaret's ancestry, to distinguish, and add distinction to, plain 'Jones', which is a relic of the patronymic ap John (son of John). Kyffin Williams used to tell a story of meeting on the road old Mrs Jones, a farmer's wife, with a pretty lamb on a lead: '"*Bore da*, Mrs Jones," I said, and (pointing to the lamb) who is this?' "Mary," said Mrs Jones. "Oh, Mary Jones is it?" I said. "No, Mary Lloyd Jones," the old lady replied.' Anyway, that 'Lloyd' figures in the name of perhaps the most famous of American architects suggests a Welsh connection. But how Welsh was he?

Richard Lloyd Jones, a small farmer and hat-maker, his wife, Mary, and their children emigrated to America in 1844. They came from south-west Wales, the parishes of Llandysul-Llanwenog, in the south of Ceredigion, close to the border with Carmarthenshire, even now a green place of small towns and smaller villages, drained by the river Teifi and its tributaries. The wave of transatlantic migration from Wales in the nineteenth century was on nothing like the scale of that from Ireland, where starvation drove people to abandon their homes in tens of thousands. A great many of the Welsh rural poor embarked on internal migration routes from homes in the west and the north of the country to the burgeoning mining valleys and steel works in the south-east, taking their language, traditions and Nonconformist religious beliefs with them. We cannot be sure what motivated Richard Lloyd Jones to risk uprooting his family for an uncertain existence far overseas. The promise of religious and political freedom may well have influenced his decision. There is every likelihood he was Liberal in politics and disadvantaged, if not persecuted, by a Tory landowner, the pattern of the times; and his religion was Unitarian. The concentration of Unitarian chapels in that part of Cardiganshire caused it to be known among detractors in the Anglican and Nonconformist chapel communities as Y Smotyn Du (the Black Spot). As late as October 1876, the local Tory bigwig was so enraged by the radical politics and Unitarian preaching of the Revd William Thomas (Gwilym Marles) that he locked him and his congregation out of Llwynrhydowen Chapel. The Revd Thomas addressed a crowd of three thousand gathered outside the locked chapel. He was Dylan Thomas's great uncle and an example of the intellectual energy of Unitarianism. Others might observe that, while it attracted great minds, like Coleridge and Ralph Waldo Emerson, it was, nonetheless, heretical.

The congregations of Y Smotyn Du were visited by that most remarkable of Welsh Unitarians, Edward Williams (Iolo Morganwg, 1750–1813), whose verses were added to tombstones in their chapel graveyards. Iolo's invention of *Gorsedd y Beirdd Ynys Prydain* (Throne of the Bards of the Island of Britain), its symbols and mottoes, rehearsed once more a few weeks ago at the National Eisteddfod in Cardiff, were (like his forged 'Dafydd ap Gwilym' poems) readily accepted by the majority Welsh-speaking population as true vestiges of a noble, unified Wales. The Lloyd Jones family carried this lore across the Atlantic, and elements of it feature repeatedly in Frank Lloyd Wright's buildings: Y gwir yn erbyn y byd (The truth against the world) and \|/, the nod cyfrin (mystic sign), the name 'Taliesin' (shining brow).

Having landed in New York, they headed for Wisconsin, where pioneering siblings from Richard's family had settled a few years before. Despite the presence of relatives, their early experience of farming a land only then beginning to emerge from wilderness may have been excruciating, as accounts by a son, Jenkin Lloyd Jones, the notable Unitarian missionary preacher, testify, but nothing dented their resolve or shrivelled their faith. It took them twelve years of trials and errors, and steady expansion of property before, in March 1856, they moved to Spring Green, and thence to Helena Valley, and a landscape reminiscent of the fields and green hills (which they named Bryn Mawr, Bryn Canol and Bryn Bach – big, middle and small hill) they had left in Wales. In 1852, Margaret, Richard's mother, aged and widowed, had written to another son in London: 'I have 30 to 40 between children and grandchildren in America living all in the same neighbourhood and close to Watertown in Wisconsin. There is a house of worship [...] where I hope they all flock on Sundays. Richard has given half an acre of land for a burial place.' It was a tribe of Welsh Joneses, living, working and worshipping together.

When they arrived in America, Frank Lloyd Wright's grandparents and their children, including Anna his mother, were more at ease in Welsh than in English. Jenkin suggests that, at least initially, his father had some difficulty in understanding English. They never lost their first language, because much of the farming day was spent in the company of those to whom Welsh came first to the mind and tongue. Even if they grew up without it, the next generation would certainly have been familiar with the shape and sounds of Welsh. Jane and Ellen (Nell), the architect's aunts, trained as teachers and, having gained valuable experience, in 1887 founded their own school in the valley where their parents had brought them and their four farming brothers. If we judge by the description of Hillside Home School in *A Goodly Fellowship*, the autobiography of Mary Ellen Chase, herself a distinguished educationalist, who taught there 1909–13, it was an extraordinarily enlightened establishment. English was, of course, the language of the school, but Y gwir yn erbyn y byd was engraved over the fireplace and Aunt Jane and Aunt Nell, as they were universally known, 'had a way of bursting into stormy Welsh to each other when some one of us [teachers] had displeased them by laziness or lack of attention to detail'.

Marriage to William Carey Wright, a music teacher, for a time took Anna away from the valley, but she returned when they separated and subsequently divorced. Young Frank, who at this point adopted the familial 'Lloyd', attended Madison High School and the University of Wisconsin-Madison, but seems not to have graduated. His training as an architect began in Chicago with the firm of J.L. Silsbee, where in 1887 he had a hand in designing the first Hillside Home School building, in the 'English' style. In 1888 he joined Adler & Sullivan as an apprentice and made rapid enough progress to accept commissions on his own account, thereby breaking the contract with his employers. In 1893 he set up on his own, and in 1901 he designed the second Hillside Home School for his aunts, in the distinctively 'Prairie' style of which he became the most famous exponent. By 1905–08, for the Unitarian Church, he had created a masterpiece, Chicago's Unity Temple.

F.L.W.'s Welsh roots are exposed for all to see; how conscious he remained of them through his long, often turbulent life is impossible to tell. He was happy to accept an Honorary Doctorate of the University of Wales at Bangor in 1956. Ah, if only the 4th Marquess of Bute had not drawn a line under his architectural ventures in Wales after funding the restoration of Caerphilly Castle, but commissioned a Frank Lloyd Wright house, in Ceredigion perhaps, as a grand gesture to the future.

Sane Artists

From the Journals, 8 March 2005

R. F. LANGLEY

Bob Walker sends me an email quoting Adam Phillips talking to Melvyn Bragg on the South Bank Show, about sane artists:

'I think one of the things we might look to poetry for now, because poetry is marginalised, which is the best thing about it... it's freeing people, actually, to be able to work in their own way. People are going to be poets now only if they really want to be, because there is no money in it and there's very little glamour. That seems to be promising: because, it seems to me, the only pay off now to being a good poet is writing a good poem, and that seems to me to hold with it the possibility that people will be freer with their thoughts. They'll be less preoccupied by being winning, or by being charming. Or indeed by selling anything, because they've got nothing to sell.

I think that the new thing that might be happening is that the new sane artist will not be seeking recognition. That whereas the main stream of artists are all going to be seeking recognition and fame and fortune, the new sane artist will need to dispense with precisely that quest in order to do their work.

It frees you, once you relinquish the market... once you relinquish, one way or another, the saleability of your art now, then you're free, I think, freer to have your own thoughts; because in so far as you're interested in marketing what you do, you have to be preoccupied by a fantasy of what people want.

So there. It feels wise. And <u>giving readings</u> is risky in the same way... it's a sort of marketability after all, especially if you begin to consider the 'normal' person, or the café audience in Halesworth. Herman is wrong to suggest the ordinary intelligent person as target audience, even. There should be no target audience, though some are worse than others – the café audience the worst possible for what I can do, I think.

What, then, of giving accounts of what you are up to? My method of reading chunks of other writers, sources, parallels etc... without much comment at all, seems the best I should do... and tomorrow I go to London to make a CD for the Poetry Archive... given the chance to introduce my poems, but, I think, turning this down and just reading, carefully, as many as I can in an hour. No marketing.

In the long run, considering how one stands vis-á-vis the lyric voice, the biographical stance, or the removal of it... is more than marketing, is it not? It is considering where you are, the good old stance towards reality, how it should be, what will suffice. So don't think I am trying to sell anything to Cambridge... in fact I am failing to do that, of course, by being 'epiphanic' or whatever, ... by still finding the robin in the garden a lot of the point.

Just heard one sing, three short bursts in the dusk, as I came back from shutting up next door's chickens. Clean and quick and very shining, in the cold, damp, muddied, broken mess of path and road and hedge. To be sane about it, then... but to do something about it that won't get a round of applause or a girl to come up afterwards to say I gave her some joy, though she 'hasn't had much joy lately'. Well... that as a bonus but not a target! Not to play for even 'comprehension' as such, I think?

[edited by Barbara Langley, August 2018]

'The Gates of Hell' and other poems

ANGE MLINKO

The Psychic Capital of the World

Cassadega, Florida

Summer. A toad died in a plastic habitat,
sparrow nestlings in the grill fledged,
the Don Juan rose's ups and downs
were managed with a spritz of sulfur at
intervals, the St Augustine was edged;
and at the crossroads of the town

there was almost nothing to trumpet
the psychic capital of the world, albeit
a unified aesthetic seemed to have bled
from a great purple pen, whose *stet*
could be read in the sign-up sheet
and hand-crafted amethyst death's head.

The dead had gone abroad while
vegetation marched on the veranda.
We imagined that they had surpassed,
by six time zones or so, a period style
on a transatlantic see-saw,
so much was our present their past –

settee, drapery, glassed-in bookshelf.
I expected a medium in a shawl
to materialise from behind
a piano – that no doubt played itself –
waving her eye of crystal
(atoms, if not planets, aligned)...

Lovers are perched on the rim of a storm.
In the gale, the Don Juan rose
thrashes a dozen siren blooms.
At the same time the rose-like form
of love's disturbance bursts windows
along the shore it hugs and dooms.

There is a legal matter to attend to;
an old pact you must put asunder.
It contributes to the rut you're in.
Is that a seagull or a sprig of mistletoe
you've managed to palely loiter under?
By summer you will cross an ocean.

The regional airport gets little traffic –
if you hear a plane, it's probably yours.
Distance would seem to abolish
the distinction between aircraft
and the bright scumble of the stars,
but a ticket goes much farther than a wish.

In your aura, no doctors or creditors.
Somewhere the sphinx moth is darting,
the clothes fall at your feet loud as snow
– who knows down what acoustic corridors?
And even the sadness of your parting
won't rise above the decibels of velcro.

The Gates of Hell

Rodin

He didn't mean these kinds of gates.
But here we are. Or I mean I.
On these darkest days of the year,
the sun shows how it accommodates
our needs, and turns itself on high.
Show me, sun, what I am doing here.

I've been thinking for some time
about 'Fallen Caryatid', shouldering
her capital. Actually there were two –
the other bore an urn; they made a rhyme.
So did *Fugit Amor*, the enduring
nature of attraction to undo.

The traveling show, arrayed in
a gallery in Savannah, was a gift.
Now at the gates of an airport,
another Christmas traveller laden
with all that should uplift,
I'm trying to be a good sport

on my first holiday without my kids.
The garbage trucks resume their rounds
on roads cellophaned with ice
masticating giftwrap like chrysalids
summarily shaken for sounds
or weighed in the hand for the size

of the happiness underneath...
I steer my thoughts back to the show
of misery beyond measurement
between gates which bequeath
images of angel wings working to slow
a fall, not manoeuvre an ascent.

The sun that cufflinks a hill's white sleeve,
the plane that bootstraps us to the sky,
neither is adequate to the human need

individual to each of us here who leave
someone else behind to cry;
queued, with scarcely a line to read.

He removed *The Kiss* from the ensemble,
surmising correctly that naked bliss
was out of place at the gates of hell.
If it *is* bliss that makes us tremble;
if it is not, also, its own abyss
between two gates at a terminal.

Possible Sea Breeze Collision in the Evening Hours

1.

A tango record's record
of scratches and scuffs
matches the dance floor's,
where women – walked backward
to 1920s Buenos Aires –
put their foot down. *His* sole buffs

the wood *her* little heel makes
half-moons in, so hard and soft
go back and forth in the atelier;
he pushes, and she brakes.
As the music carries them aloft,
all of life seems statelier.

Now, this composer knew a myth
is the simplest amplifier;
stoking his fangirls' flame,
he hid the woman he was with
out of the line of fire
in a secret hacienda; laid claim

to Uruguay as native land and muse;
avowed that his mother was a widow.
But she was an unmarried *fille*.
A record of his birth exists in Toulouse.
All of which must go to show
the better stories tend to be iffy,

the three-minute arias ring true –
if three minutes is about how long
we can hold our breath;
and for all the dancing à deux
we hand each other off for a song,
digging in our heels at death.

2.

Cheek by jowl, these subdivisions
live amongst the remnants
of the farms they have replaced.
Tongue in cheek, the signage runs
Rip van Winkle Ranch,
with no real sense of haste.

A grazing bull would stand
in its paddock, undisturbed

by the main road – until
'Bull for sale: one grand'
meant that he'd been served,
and eventually went spectral.

The day of the full eclipse
milling crescents in the shadows,
we sat on a bench and saw
only each other; then the tips
of a bull's horns, in twos,
charged everything with awe.

Heaven's china shop might be
stampeded by those wraiths
as the celestial plates aligned.
It was the last thing some would see;
blame solar retinopathy
for the thing that made us blind.

3.

A ship loaded with cattle, en route
from Uruguay to Syria, sank
that December near Beirut –
each wave trying to outrank
the last before slamming the sea wall
with the vast surge of a cattle call.

At the picture window, I watched.
What did I expect: that cows
would rebound from the surf,
rescuing themselves, patched
from tankers and scows
and give themselves up for beef?

A few miles south, Jove hid
in a bull (what is myth trying to tell us?).
Our labyrinthine lives, hybrid
of economy and transport,
are enough to make me jealous
for when we were gods' sport...

I could see the neon hotel sector
where convoys were brought to bear
on headland curves; the deck chairs
cleared for milongas; nectar
of night blooms in the hair
advancing international affairs.

Unclean and Untidy:
Notes on Graves, Myth and European War

A lecture delivered at the 14th Robert Graves Society Conference, Palma de Mallorca, 12 July 2018

Sean O'Brien

LADIES AND GENTLEMEN: not for the first time, I need to tread warily where many experts are assembled. So let me say first that I'm not a scholar and not a Graves expert. I am an interested reader of Graves's work. I have a poet's interest in Graves's writing, and the criticism I write – this talk included – emerges from a poet's preoccupations. In this instance, I began thinking about a couple of famous Graves poems arising from the First World War. I found that they met up with other parts of my reading and writing on the matter of Europe, and I've begun – barely begun, as will become evident – to explore where these connections might lead. I make no claims to originality; I'm trying to find my way to a destination which remains uncertain. So the title is accurate: these are notes.

In the *Histories* Herodotus finds that there are certain things he cannot get to the bottom of – such as the names and definitions of the continents known to the ancient world. He comments:

> As for Europe, nobody knows if it is surrounded by sea, or where it got its name from, or who gave it, unless we are to say that it came from Europa, the Tyrian woman, and before that was nameless like the rest. This, however, is unlikely; for Europa was an Asiatic and never visited the country which we now call Europe [...] But that is quite enough on this subject [.]

Herodotus's unsatisfied enquiries evoke that most imaginatively useful and appealing state, 'time out of mind', where human agency shades back into prehistory and/or theology. One of the most important features of Europe, our present subject (yet one that perhaps is sometimes taken for granted or viewed as merely obvious) is that it cannot be exhaustively known or described: it holds more than we can ever know; its existence, perhaps especially for those of an imaginative disposition, depends (for good and ill) on its capacity to escape or exceed definition. It is to an incalculable degree made up of fiction. The myth-making inclination, or at any rate the capacity for absorbing and realising or reifying myth, is present in nearly all of us. We depend on it; we live by it; it is an imaginative as well as a cultural and a political necessity, and the Greek myths about which Robert Graves wrote so copiously (and, it is said, imaginatively) have been a major shaping influence on what we have become. They continue to be so even as educated people forget them or never learn about them.

In the First World War, the language and imagery of British propaganda and nationalism unsurprisingly emphasise the menacing otherness of the Germans, their alleged brutality, cynicism and cunning, their treachery against civilised standards (recalling the betrayal of the Romans in the massacre at Teutoberg in AD 9 by the German-born general Arminius). As a child I was given a stack of magazines, *The Great War*, which had been published weekly throughout the conflict. I was too young to read the text, but the images have stayed with me all my life, particularly one lurid drawing of a German machine-gun team firing from the back of what purports to be a Red Cross ambulance. Especially in the early days of the war, great emphasis was placed on the Germans' unhesitating barbarism. Robert Graves was to withdraw from these assumptions, but something related does surface in one of his most interesting and eerie poems, 'A Dead Boche', written after he entered Mametz Wood during the battle of the Somme, an episode that recurs in *Goodbye to All That*. Here's the poem:

> To you who'd read my songs of War
> And only hear of blood and fame,
> I'll say (you've heard it said before)
> 'War's Hell!' and if you doubt the same,
> Today I found in Mametz Wood
> A certain cure for lust of blood:
>
> Where, propped against a shattered trunk
> In a great mess of things unclean,
> Sat a dead Boche: he scowled and stunk
> With clothes and face a sodden green,
> Big-bellied, spectacled, crop-haired,
> Dribbling black blood from nose and beard.

Graves is in fact keen to distinguish between vulgar patriotic uplift and the seemingly plain grim facts of the aftermath of battle. Jean Moorcroft Wilson in her new biography of Graves notes the poem's 'punchy, realistic description' but adds that 'A Dead Boche' is 'by no means representative of Graves's war poetry, which depends mainly on a more indirect approach through myth, legend and ancient history'. Certainly when the poem first caught my attention is was the apparent matter-of-factness which interested me. Moorcroft Wilson adds that the poem 'came to represent for many a typical war poem by Graves'. I was also struck by the absence of a resolving conclusion to the poem: the 'facts' were left to speak for themselves. 'A Dead Boche' (along with the 'The Untidy Man', which I will look at briefly later on) has continued to fascinate me, but now, as far as 'A Dead Boche' is concerned, it seems as if the 'punchy realism' is itself rooted in and dependent on myth, legend and ancient history.

In his recent book *The Shortest History of Germany*, James Hawes writes about the myth of Germany, and the way its moves towards unification expose a fundamental insecurity both in and beyond the emergent German nation, a separation of realms between what lies west and east of the Rhine (and later, east of the Elbe). This was a matter of concern to the Romans. It figures in Tacitus's *Annals*, and the slaughter of the three legions led by Varus by the German tribes under the turncoat Arminius, a German who had become a Roman general, at Teutoberg in Lower Saxony in A D 9 has not yet ceased to carry a fearful imaginative resonance. Hawes's brisk, absorbing, entertaining book offers an impatient pragmatism, an underlying realism, but in the end he too is a myth-maker, with a myth founded in geography and river systems, whereby geography is destiny. The place gives rise to myth; the myth defines the place; place and myth come to feel inseparable.

This sense of threat has its place in the hinterland of Graves's poem.

In the first stanza he offers his readers a chance to set aside sentimental mythologising notions of 'blood and fame'; in the second he concentrates on a single casualty. Yet in doing so he invokes a more enduring myth – the German in the wood, his greenness ('Boche' seemingly derived from the French 'caboche', cabbage) making the German soldier part of the setting, even, or perhaps especially, in death; a physically real yet anonymous figure, menacing even though lifeless, for 'scowled' and 'stank' are active verbs: as Charles Mundye observes in his edition of Graves's war poems, they are things the dead Boche impossibly does. In his First World War memoir *Storm of Steel* (*In Stahlgewittern*, 1920), Ernst Junger describes an action at the beginning of the Battle of the Somme, and then its aftermath, from the German viewpoint. The translation is by Michael Hofman:

> The day's sentries were already in position while the trenches had yet to be cleared. Here and there, the sentry posts were covered with dead, and in among them, as it were, arisen from their bodies, stood the new relief with his rifle. There was an odd rigidity about these composites – it was as though the distinction between live and dead had momentarily been taken away.

We are inescapably reminded of Graves's own 'resurrection' after his death was announced following the action at High Wood, and of the traffic between life and death in 'To Bring the Dead to Life'. The mythological possibilities of combat are meat and drink to Junger's martial aestheticism. Perhaps he would have understood and assented to Thomas Mann's contention in *Refelctions of a Non-Political Man* that 'art has a basically undependable, treacherous tendency; its joy in scandalous unreason, its tendency to beauty-creating "barbarism", cannot be rooted out'. Over and above the 'normal' reactions Junger displays – loss, comradeship, and mercy – something about the 'infernal carnival' of bombardment and slaughter seduces and exalts him. He is always ready to stand in the trench, 'flame-capped' like Achilles, ready for combat. During the Allied bombardment of Fresnoy (situated between Agincourt and Crècy), he invites us to see him at the window of a house, like Goethe pictured at a window in Rome on his Italian journey. He comments: 'peeping over Destiny's shoulder like that to see her hand, it's easy to become negligent and risk one's own life.' It's a moment that foreshadows his excited observation, in his journals, of an Allied air-raid on Paris in the Second World War, which he witnessed from the roof of the hotel where he was billeted:

> I held in my hand a glass of burgundy with strawberries floating in it. The city with its red towers and domes lay stretched out in breathtaking beauty like a chalice that is overflown for deadly pollination. Everything was spectacle, pure power, affirmed and exalted by pain.

There is an ingrained, framing sense of culture, of cultural purpose and role in these observations – a perspective which seems quite alien to Graves, whose suggestion that people ought to be expected to have read an agreed number of approved books seems modest in comparison.

Graves's response in 'A Dead Boche' is more controlled and restrained, the horrors of the scene present yet not relished. But the dead German seems as much a figure from the Teutoberg Forest, and from the unnamed, uncanny, ubiquitous Forest of folktale and fairytale, Perrault and Grimm, as from the woodlands of the Somme after their reduction to splinters between 7–12 July 1916. The German forces present in Mametz Wood were, it seems, the 11/2 Lehr regiment of the Prussian Guard. This unit was, in martial terms, the elite, the real, battle-hardened thing – experienced, resourceful, durable, resolute, like their remote Germanic ancestors. (The very name of Prussia itself was acquired by association from the people with whom German knights did battle in the east.) The troops in Mametz Wood, then, are certainly not to be underrated as those ancestors were by Varus, who is said to have entered the Teutoberg Forest without assuming battle formation. The Welsh attack on Mametz Wood had a formation, but its tactics proved just as suicidal as those of the Roman general, though Haig criticised the Welsh's 'lack of push'.

Mametz Wood itself after the battle contains what Graves calls 'a great mess of things unclean'. Readers can hardly avoid the background echo – and the sentimental dissonance – of 'swimmers into cleanness leaping' in Rupert Brooke's famous anticipatory poem 'The Soldier'. Cleanliness, according to John Wesley, is next to godliness. It is often flanked by tidiness. Graves transposes terms in common domestic use to a grotesquely inappropriate context, with an implied rebuke to those safely, cleanly, tidily at home in England, who can hardly imagine the real conditions of the conflict. So much for 'cleanness'. Meanwhile, though, the term 'unclean' seems almost to have lapsed from ordinary usage; insofar as it is familiar it tends to arise in the context of religious dietary observance (the pig being of course considered an 'unclean' animal in the Old Testament, in Deuteronomy and Leviticus). The OED offers 'morally wrong' and 'evil' among the word's meanings, and in the context of the poem these senses are also suggestively present. Evil, according to the OED, is associated with ritual. We may read the battle just ended, and its consequences, as aspects of ritual, in this instance a practice invoking or involving hallowed powers but not, it seems, the possibility of redemption. It is possible to read the line as balanced between the casual and the sacerdotal: 'a great mess', where 'mess' underplays the evidence of the slaughter in the wood; but 'mess' too pertains to food, both as a substance and the place where, for example, soldiers eat when not in combat. It also means 'confusion or muddle', of course, and this sense leads back to the idea of a dish which is 'liquid or pulpy', like the Biblical 'mess of potage', and perhaps even prepared for an animal rather than a human to eat. We are supping full of horrors when we contemplate the wood; it is a shambles of bodies and body parts. It is an 'unnatural scene', something we prefer to consider inhuman, displaying a loss of physical definition, something outside our repertoire of act and sensation. Mametz Wood as Graves finds it insists on the brute physical reality of 'life' after shot, shell and bayonet, where men have behaved 'like animals' while treating their opponents as less than human. As Tacitus tells us in the *Annals*, when, several years after Teutoberg, Roman forces reached the site of battle they found evidence of terrifying atrocities, committed seemingly in ritual form:

> In the center of the field were the whitening bones of men, as they had fled, or stood their ground, strewn everywhere or piled in heaps. Near lay fragments of weapons and limbs of horses, and also human heads, prominently nailed to trunks of trees. In the adjacent groves were the barbarous altars, on which they had immolated tribunes and first-rank centurions.
>
> Some survivors of the disaster who had escaped from the battle or from captivity, described how this was the spot where the officers fell, how yonder the eagles were captured, where Varus was pierced by his first wound, where too by the stroke of his own ill-starred hand he found for himself death. They pointed out too the raised ground from which Arminius had harangued his army, the number of gibbets for the captives, the pits for the living, and how in his exultation he insulted the standards and eagles.

Graves, we might infer, could reasonably expect contemporary readers to have known, or at any rate to have internalised, something of the etymologies of the key terms. They combine with each other to produce an image half-abstracted from what it gestures towards, inclined to restraint but also needing to secure our understanding of what it does not plainly state. We might see this as a form of imaginative self-preservation on the poet's part, even as it seeks to set the brute facts before the reader. Strangely, it seems that no sooner have we encountered an 'objective', relatively dispassionate description, than we are overtaken by myth.

The poem's combination of grotesquerie and discretion in presenting a sense of involuntary immersion, from which the observer/poet recoils into a controlled and tactful description, is emphasised if we compare Graves's poem with Keith Douglas's 1943 poem 'Vergissmeinnicht'. There, 'returning over the nightmare ground' three weeks after the battle, the speaker offers a description in which the dead German gunner is no longer 'there' – witness 'the paper eye', and the 'burst stomach like a cave'. Douglas's effort of detachment lends power to the closing paradox whereby the dead man is both killer and lover (there is a photo nearby, inscribed: Steffi: Vergissmeinnicht). For Douglas, there are no comebacks; while for Graves the dead Boche has not really gone away. Douglas's imagination, despite the 'nightmare' of the setting, imparts a kind of decisive 'cleanliness' to the 'mess' of conflict. His poem, for all its mythic paradox, seems part of the way to demythologising the subject in favour of the material facts: the dead man's equipment is 'hard and good when he's decayed'. What all of Douglas's mature poetry discounts is the future; plagued by the black rider Care, he awaits what seems, and proved to be, his certain death.

The extinction of the future and with it the extinction of myth are also conspicuous in the work of the German novelist Gert Ledig. In the opening passage of his 1955 novel *The Stalin Organ*, we see how things might look when the possibility of myth is excluded once and for all, leaving nihilism to mop up. The episode takes places on the Leningrad Front in 1941. The translation is again by Michael Hofmann:

> The Lance-Corporal couldn't turn in his grave, because he didn't have one. Some three versts from Podrova, forty versts south of Leningrad, he had been caught in a salvo of rockets, been thrown up in the air, and with severed hands and head dangling, been impaled on the skeletal branches of what once had been a tree.
>
> The NCO, who was writhing on the ground with a piece of shrapnel in his belly, had no idea what was keeping his machine-gunner. It didn't occur to him to look up. He had his hands full with himself.
>
> The two remaining members of the unit ran off, without bothering about their NCO. If someone had later told them they should have made an effort to fetch the Lance-Corporal down from his tree, they would quite rightly have said he had a screw loose. The Lance-Corporal was already dead, thank God. Half an hour later, when the crippled tree trunk was taken off an inch or two above the ground by a burst of machine-gun fire, his wrecked body came down anyway. In the intervening time, he had also lost a foot. The frayed sleeves of his tunic were oily with blood. By the time he hit the ground he was just half a man.

The tone here is laconic, the attitude, the irony, one might say, endemic, 'professional' – 'The Lance-Corporal was already dead, thank God'. The passage closes on a note of nihilistic humour. We are a long way from 'swimmers into cleanness leaping', a long way from the warrior-aesthete mythos of Junger, and from the resonant tact of Robert Graves. Such is the book's disenchantment that there is almost no position to occupy in relation to Ledig's material, and the margin of humour is not for anybody. Ledig's was a voice not wholly welcome in Germany when it was published in 1955. But his work reads as a template for the attitude to war taken in innumerable books and films since: unshockably cynical, nihilistic, not to be trapped into feeling. In his introduction to *The Stalin Organ*, Michael Hofmann remarks that while the book is about chaos, it is thoroughly designed, with 'the intricacy almost of farce in its operation'. Its realism is of course literary, selective, aware of figure and ground, tone and structure. In this respect it differs from a day-to-day combat journal such as that kept by Hans Roth, a corporal in an anti-tank unit, who served on the Russian Front from the opening of Operation Barbarossa in 1941 until his disappearance in action in 1944 during the collapse of Wehrmacht Group Centre. It was published as *Eastern Inferno: the Journals of a German Panzerjäger*.

Roth's account of combat is accomplished, vivid, horrific and apparently unfiltered; the Russian Front is a machine for turning men into meat, and the three volumes of his diary chart the gradual worsening of conditions as the Wehrmacht begins to lose the war. He could never have got the material past the Wehrmacht's censors and the journal can hardly have been intended for a readership. There is no oversight, no detached perspective. His frequent loving references to his wife and child are juxtaposed with a blend of contemptuous hatred for the Russian enemy, who he complains don't fight properly like the French but go on without regard for casualties, and grudging admiration of their skills. Roth is complicit in atrocity at times – the execution of prisoners is accepted as 'what must be done', even as he sympathises with the plight of civilians. He witnesses the mass murder of Jews and finds it unconscionable, wondering how the men who keenly commit the slaughter will be able to live as civilians with families when the war is over. Roth's viewpoint has almost no explicit history and its spoken ideology is largely a romantic affirmation of love and the landscapes of home, alternating with a received mythological sense of German cultural and military exceptionalism, the texture of which is thin compared with the day-to-day reality of the war. He records his own incoherence, the threat of breakdown from unrelieved front-line exposure balanced against his refusal when wounded to leave the men in his section. He seems, as it were, more or less demythologised. Whatever cultural inheritance he shares is failing and deserting him. At one point Roth instructs himself: 'Don't think, Hannes, for heaven's sake, don't think!'

W. G. Sebald's *On the Natural History of Destruction* surveys German writing in the immediate post-war period, looking for work which tackles the destruction wrought on German cities by the allied aerial bombing campaign. The firestorm raids on Hamburg and Dresden – a kind and degree of destruction hitherto impossible (though by no means unimaginable) – recall that phrase used by Ernst Junger to describe the experience of bombardment on the Western Front: an 'infernal carnival'. What Sebald finds is that the subject is avoided, suppressed, set aside as post-war rebuilding begins. For the most part he condemns the few books he finds as evasive, sentimental, fraudulently metaphysical, weirdly aggrandised, self-exculpatory, and, we note, sometimes hungry for restorative myth. Taking Hermann Kasack's *Die Stadt hinter dem Strom* (*The City Beyond the River*, 1947) as a key text of the period, he observes that the mystical fantasy of eastward expansion to facilitate rebirth 'shows with alarming clarity that the secret language supposedly cultivated by "internal emigrants" was to a high degree identical with the code of the Fascist intellectual world.' We might wonder at his surprise at the eschewal of realism: 'humankind cannot bear very much reality', as Eliot observed, and, to paraphrase Geoffrey's Hill's words in his essay on Funeral Music, the prospect of Germany bombed flat seems likely to have beggared description. What Sebald seeks are objective accounts of how Germany looked, felt and smelt; by and large, he says, these are not to be found. Any such survey must be incomplete. Ledig, another of whose books, *Payback*, deals with the Allied bomber raids, is made an honourable exception, as is Peter Weiss. For the rest, for some time much of the history of the period seems to have been shut away or cut off from itself: it is not only the victims who suffer trauma (Hans Roth wondered in horror what the 'normal' post-war lives of those who murdered Jews would be like). And if you cannot bear to think, there is always value in activity: best to be doing, sweeping the streets, tending the vegetable garden while the rubble is slowly cleared and the smell of corpses fades.

But whether involuntary or willed, amnesia is eventually rejected by some, though not necessarily in identical ways. Memory, or its effacement, contributes to the rage embodied in the Baader Meinhof Group in the 1970s – whose aims the passage of time makes increasingly difficult to understand – to the point where it seems that terror became an end in itself, as if the only position available was violent revolt whose true object was to perpetuate itself in gestures of immolation and Wagnerian treason. It seems that even at the extremes of a kind of Marxism, myth, or more than one myth, was stirring. Hans Kundnani's book *Utopia or Auschwitz* studies the German generation of 1968 in revolt against their parents' conduct in war and peace, and against their Americanised material complacency. One of the book's most fascinating elements is the movement of some extreme leftists to the extreme right, as in the case of Horst Mahler, an early opponent of immigration. Another is the helpless attempt by Rudi Dutschke, the German student leader, survivor of an assassination attempt, to go round rather than work through the Holocaust, on the grounds that to contemplate it would enfeeble political hope. In the Historikerstreit of 1986–89, whatever their claims to rationality, the attempts, led by Ernst Nolte, to relativise the Holocaust, absolve Germany of guilt and assert the right to forget (!), suggest the resurgence of myth as an act of moral sanitation. The attempt to dispose of myths seems to end in their regeneration in transmuted form, as negations – myths at some level akin to Mann's description of art: 'its joy in scandalous unreason, its tendency to beauty-creating "barbarism", cannot be rooted out.' Perhaps, behind it all, lies the appeal of the death-cult, most recently embodied in Nazism.

I seem to have moved a long way from 'A Dead Boche', but Graves, more than most writers, understood the necessity of myth, of the mysterious coherence with which it can accommodate love, violence and horror. These are, in Empson's words, 'Ambiguous gifts, as what gods give must be': to acknowledge them is also to have to reckon with them. Lastly, I move on to 'The Untidy Man', an uncollected poem written at some point between 1918 and 1927. The setting is domestic, with a sense of the nursery and a nursery rhyme form, and again the unlikely, the uncanny and the unclean are present, while the tone is matter-of-fact:

There was a man, a very untidy man,
Whose fingers could nowhere be found to put in his tomb.
He had rolled his head far underneath the bed:
He had left his legs and arms lying all over the room.

Given the context of war, it is not a surprising coincidence that Ernst Junger should have encountered something not dissimilar:

I saw a basement flattened... Near the entrance one man lay on his belly in a shredded uniform: his head was off, and the blood had flowed into a puddle. When an ambulanceman turned him over to check him for valuables, I saw as in a nightmare that his thumb was still hanging from the remnants of his arm.

This scene – more deliberately explicit than Graves in 'A Dead Boche' – cannot help but bring to mind Struwwelpeter and the Scissor-man, figures from the horrifying children's poems by Heinrich Hoffmann (1845) – which was also, in a coincidence both eerie and banal, the name of Hitler's personal photographer. In Hoffman's poems the punishment far outstrips the crime. These were poems which Graves's German mother seems likely to have given him to read, for example 'The Story of Little Suck-a-Thumb':

> The door flew open, in he ran,
> The great, long, red-legged Scissorman.
> Oh! children, see! the tailor's come
> And caught our little Suck-a-Thumb.
> Snip! Snap! Snip! the scissors go;
> And Conrad cries out – Oh! Oh! Oh!
> Snip! Snap! Snip! They go so fast;
> That both his thumbs are off at last.

Domesticity is often the home of terror and horror, as the mundane is transformed by the coming of night into a theatre of bad dreams. The 'long, red-legged Scissorman' rushes in with his giant tailors' shears. Graves, we know, was drawn to childhood and wrote poems addressed to children and showing a surviving child's-eye view in himself. In 'The Untidy Man', though, the character seems not to be an untidy, careless child – who would, as the saying has it, lose his head if it wasn't screwed on, but a grown man. But if the child is father to the man, here he still lives within the man, with a child's perspective and imaginative magnification and vulnerability. Now he must almost be crammed back into the child-sized space for which this kind of story might be imagined by Hans Andersen. Sebald refers to German refugees in an episode observed by Friedrich Reck in Bavaria in 1943, where 'a cardboard suitcase bursts open, revealing "Toys, a manicure case, singed underwear. And last of all, the roasted corpse of a child, preserved like a mummy"' – or like something terrifying in a fairytale, and dead but not quite dead.

Graves's untidy man has somehow come apart into his component sections, like a giant doll. Disassembled, he is both there and not there. Being a man, he is to be buried in a tomb (as the suitcase is the tomb of the mummified child, and though like the dead Boche the untidy man does not seem exactly dead). The 'room' must serve as his tomb – with perhaps a background suggestion that the room is an officers' dugout in a trench. 'Tomb' has gravity, grandeur, a sense of posterity, but also in this context an air of absurd aggrandisement: tombs are for kings and generals, not anonymous 'men' like this, or for children, and yet the untidy man is subject to and included in the governing narrative. The horror and pathos of the poem, and the sense of being in the presence of a madness which is cultural and collective rather than individual, show meaning at once destroyed and restored, the myth rising again to contain contradictions otherwise insupportable.

At the level of character, two founding texts of European literature, *The Iliad* and *The Odyssey*, encompass huge contradictions in human behaviour – Hector's heroism and his fear of the final encounter with Achilles; Achilles' ferocity and his love for Patroclus; Ulysses' wanton slaughter of the housemaids – by seeing these contradictions as founding facts of human behaviour. As soon as morality enters the frame, such matters have to be scrutinised and accounted for in a different way. In some cases, military valour and loyalty are seen as the noblest of aspirations (see Vigny's *A Soldier's Life*) with commitment to a tribe, a regiment, a platoon or an emperor – something bigger than the self, as a kind of proxy for morality. We find this commitment in both Graves and Junger, but where Junger embraces battle as a sort of metaphysical and artistic privilege (and goes on doing so into the Second World War), Graves has to find another route, another mythological path to making sense, whereby, perhaps, violence itself seems to be transformed into the challenge and ordeal of love and the erotic life. Both writers are mythologists: both see myth as a necessity, and the myths they turn to (in Junger's case, in the curiously inert fantasy *On the Marble Cliffs*), both arise as though from the back of the mind of Europe, Europa, a place as much in need and fear of the power of myth as ever, a place which we cannot understand, and will not be able to save, if we do not recognise that it consists as much of myth as reality. It is the great and terrible work of the imagination which we have no choice but to serve, for good or ill. As Thom Gunn put it in his poem 'Adolescence', we are 'part, still, of the done war'. Europe cannot be understood in its entirety; but it cannot be understood at all if it is not seen as a work of the imagination.

Mapping the Woods

REBECCA HURST

'... woods are evidently places propitious for wandering,
or getting lost in, all woods are a sort of labyrinth.'
— *Francis Ponge,* The Notebook of the Pine Woods

Parson's Wood, Mayfield, East Sussex
Longitude: 51.061001; Latitude: 0.308827

I. Winter solstice

(21 December 2009
sunrise: 08.00 am
sunset: 03.54 pm)

Between dark and dusk
we walk to the brink of the year,
an iron-red line on cinereous clay.

Hands cramp with cold on the old road
as we sketch and note this half-hour
past sunrise but not brightening
though the rooks are awake and jigging
on the frosted shoulders of a broad oak.

Pass a nip of brandy, roll another smoke.
Make a mark
and a mark   on the damp page.

This winter's day the wood is a room,
screened by snow, shuttered and barred,
                                        nothing doing.
Yes, we feel the Parson's coppiced acres,
feel the challeybeate and charcoal in our bones.

Three walkers, we beat the bounds,
talking of other pilgrimages:
the vixen's path
                    the vole's path
                            the roebuck's.

From the knap of this hill the wood
is perspicuous. It holds a pose:
the line of golden larches, the net
of branches the beech casts to the sky.

Count the ways in:
the tracks and driftways,
sheere-ways and stiles,
the bostals and tripets,
gaps, twittens and stiles.
Loop round and back again.
These Wealden hills burn us up –
the effort of taking them in the snow.

Fumbling in pockets for a pencil stub
I trace the shape of a chestnut bole,
a rosette of reindeer moss.
The doctor's lanky son peers down,
says, 'Cla-cla-donia rangiferina,'
and harrups to clear his throat.
Rolls another smoke.
Siân hands out gold chocolate coins,
blows her cold-pinked nose.

By the hammer pond we peer
through the burne-washed brick tunnel.
The water races, black as slate.
Three centuries back there was a foundry
here: a pond bay, trough and furnace.
We light a cardboard waterwheel.
It doubles, spins and crackles.
The old year creaks, then turns
as with a flash the flames ignite
quick as the robin flits
across the ice-fringed pool.

Night comes early.
We set a candle in the window.
There is stew in the oven,
wine and bread and salt on the table.
Johnny draws back the curtains
and St George ambles
through the unlocked door.
We cheer as he slays the Turk
with his righteous sword,
cheer again when the dead
man is magicked back to life.

Walking home through the wood
an hour past midnight
I find a chestnut leaf
                lying on the path,
                            fallen
picked up
                    then palmed

between the pages of this notebook.

II. Spring equinox

(20 March 2010
 sunrise: 06.03 am
 sunset: 06.10 pm)

Sugar moon, stiff hands flexing.
Station Street to High Street
down Fletching Street to Coggin's Mill.
The air is tepid and thick,
mist draws down along
the sandstone ridge.
Traffic reporting from the A26.
Birdsong quadraphonic;
simulcasting spring.
I feel it too.
Yawn, warming
as I walk, and
my body yields.

At Johnny's house a bedroom window
is propped open. We shout in the dark,
'Wake up lapsy!' and a lean shadow
calls, 'Good morning! Be right down.'
We take a thermos of tea, fill our pockets
with Simnel cake and tie our bootlaces tight.

6.04 am. A minute past the day's dawning
but no sun. Just grey cloud and the clatter
of the burne, rain-choked and precipitate.

We circle the rough-sketched
woodland, walking in silence.

Downstream from the hammer pond
we paddle along a reach of gravel.
Above us the bank rises ten feet sheer.
We dig in the clay for nuggets
of charcoal, slag and ore,
grubbing out a lump of iron
big as my head. It is cast
with foliage, a dainty kissing ball
made of lion's mouth, celandine,
hemlock and stitchwort.

Later we sit in a row on a gate
and Johnny tells a story
he heard from Alf Clout –

'There was a white bullock
round as the moon
who broke a fence
and lost himself deep
in this tangled thicket.
He dwells here still,
and each year in March
there's one who will see him.
And they're in for a hard year,
poor soul, for a glimpse
of the white stot bodes ill.'

We nod, make note and eat our sandwiches.

Twelve hours pass in doing
not much
but walking and watching the shift
in shade and tone on this sunless day.

We wash our hands and drink from the spring,
tie three-dozen ribbons to the ash tree
that sprouts nearby –
a wish for every bright strip of cloth
binding us close to this crooked place.

The flat light drains colour from the fields,
submerges the intricacies of the wood
and exhausts the gaze. Nightfall
revives the faded landscape
just as it begins to rain
and we see the gleaming bones
of a long-dead oak and the bronze
and mauve of budding trees.

Still walking, homeward now, heads down
against the rain, ready to see this bout through,
we cover the conifer plantation
make our last lap along the Little Rother.

Mud licks our boots. We walk blind
night-fallen, surefooted. Until
the path dips and there is a flurry
like a leaf turning in the breeze.

Siân stops.
        Peers down.
'A toad', she calls out in warning
and summoning
for then there is a frog and a frog
and another toad
and five, six, seven more
leaping up from beneath our feet
green and gold on grey.

We walk   single file
                 heads bowed
                 and counting our steps
                 with care
                 on this most lively road
                 through the woods
                 knowing

they've woken to warmth and dark
and wriggled from their muddy holes
to mate in the puddles and ponds
where they were spawned.

We hear them crooning now
for this damp gloaming
is their unimaginable high noon
and the wet
and the warmth
and the woods
have called
and they have come.

III. Summer solstice

(21 June 2010
  sunrise: 04.44 am
  sunset: 09.17 pm)

Milk thistle is the solitary maid
settling her spindle in the coppice
amongst the chestnut boles
and bee-fingered foxgloves.

The stream is silent, stretching
itself from blue sunrise to last light,
seventeen hours long. No rush then.

And the leaf canopy is a bold new green,
while fireweed and knapweed,
ragwort and buttercup scald
the fields and verges and tracts
of common ground.

We follow a fox-track flush
with orchids and milk-maids,
make tea from pods of Solomon's seal,
inhale the rare steam and lie about
in the long grass waiting
and reading aloud.

Johnny unpacks the picnic:
bread, cheese, tomatoes
red as my sun-flushed face,
Milton's *Comus*,
a dish of watercress,
another of strawberries.

Taking off his shirt and tilting his hat,
the doctor's son begins to read:

    The first Scene discovers a wild wood.
The ATTENDANT SPIRIT descends or enters.

Afternoon dozing –

    I dream of a woman
    sitting with her lap full
    of some puzzle of yarn.

She wears green and gold
and is all pins and needles,
bobbins, hooks and barbs.

She reaches out and snips
a slit in the day with tiny brass scissors.
The sun slides through the tear

And wake to see the runic heron
tow its long legs across the sky.
Rooks follow, black ribbons
unspooling.

It is time then
and we take tea-lights
to the hammer pond
while night seeps in
        like a promise half-kept

and we light the dish of black water.

Now this small place
is an amphitheatre,
the stories we tell in whispers, epic.

    Siân spins a yarn:

The way she tells it,
the scraggly milk thistle
moves at night
on tattered feet. I believe
she has that in her,
to tear herself from the soil,
        to creep
    close,
    closer.

And at daybreak to replant her feet
in charcoal and clay,
far from home
and back again.

IV. Autumn equinox

(23 September 2010
 sunrise: 06.47 am
 sunset: 06. 57 pm)

The rosebay willowherb
has gone to spume.
Siân, leading the way,
finds a great web
blocks our path.
The spider – a stripy-legged man –
hovers in the corner of his larder-loom.

We have been out for an hour.
The birds are rousing.
My stomach growls.
I pick blackberries.
A hazel leaf shivers
                and drops.

This wood was full of children
when I was young.
We built dens using cut branches
the men who came to coppice
left behind. And in the charcoal
pits lit fires, cooked our tea –
cans of beans and sausages.
We came here with matches
and small dogs
homemade bows and arrows
and paper boats
and penny chews.
We skinny-dipped
in the hammer pond,
stayed out too late,
let the glow worms
light us home.

I knew all the old stories:
dragons and devils,
saints and sweeps,
tusked wild boar,
the white bull lost
and still looking
for a way through.
At night sometimes
tucked up in bed
I heard him roar.

And yet for all that
the wood let us enter
and saw us leave
to live our lives,
grow up,
move away.

Now I think on it
there were only three of us
playing in the wood.
Sister, friend and me.
Now three again
constructing a sukkah
of willow and bracken.
Lying inside we look up,
see the tawny autumn
leaves and the blue sky.

Later I sit on an oak limb
shaggy with lichen.
The air is warm
on my bare arms.

I feel just right,
                at home
here in my skin
and in the woods,
up to my ankles
in leaf-mould
and sphagnum moss.

Beyond
the clamour of insects
rises in waves and rolls down
the sun-struck meadow.
The shrilling fills the wood
like a hive brewing to swarm.

And yes, I hear you calling.
I take off my shoes.
Remember we said
we'd walk home barefoot?
The ground is warm
and turning.

Borders & Crossings: Varieties of Exile

Presented at the 14th Robert Graves Conference in Palma, Mallorca, on 12 July 2018

Richard Gwyn

Once near a border, it is impossible not to be involved, not to want to exorcise or transgress something. Just by being there, the border is an invitation. Come on, it whispers, step across this line. If you dare. To step across the line, in sunshine or under cover of night, is fear and hope rolled into one [...] People die crossing borders, and sometimes just being near them. The lucky ones are reborn on the other side.

— Kapka Kassabova

BORDERS DEFINE US and deny us; they carve out entire tracts of the planet, reward those born by chance within certain territories, and condemn others to a condition of otherness and anomie. Crossing borders is, for much of the world's population, an act of transgression and often involves huge risk.

Borders not only shape lives; they serve a political purpose by promoting a sense of insider and outsider, of belonging and of exile. But perhaps exile itself is a kind of belonging, the forging of an outsider identity that involves, as Kassabova notes, being reborn.

Roberto Bolaño said – rather ungraciously, perhaps – on being invited to speak on the theme of Literature and Exile: 'I don't believe in exile, especially not when the word sits next to the word 'literature'.' And I can see his point: unless you are Aleksandr Solzhenitsyn or Taslima Nasreen (or even Ovid) few writers are threatening or influential enough to be exiled specifically for what they write, although they may – and in some parts of the world still are – beaten to death or poisoned or imprisoned for long years. A brief scan of PEN International's register of imprisoned or missing writers will confirm that.

But exile? When and how do writers find themselves in exile? Wole Soyinka has written: 'When is exile?... Where is exile? Is there a state of exile? For surely even an exile must exist in some space physical and mental.' There is even, he claims, a strong temptation to describe exile as simply a state of mind.

And here it is useful to reflect on the voluntary exile associated with writers such as James Joyce, Lawrence Durrell, Robert Graves and many others, whose self-banishment might be expressed in terms of a kind of disgust born of over-familiarity with aspects of the homeland that make it impossible to remain. Exile of this kind might be explained in the terms chosen by Soyinka – by his own admission, whimsically and only half-seriously – as 'the true temperament of the writer or the artist tribe in general: a creature in a permanent state of exile, since his or her real vocation is the eradication of the barriers of reality.' In a strange way, this reminds me of Alastair Reid's concept of the 'foreigner' – of which anonymity is a crucial component: 'Anonymity is peculiarly appealing to a foreigner: he is always trying to live in a nowhere, in the complex of his present.' The anonymity of the foreigner is cognate with the detachment of the exile:

From there, if they are lucky, they smuggle back occasional undaunted notes, like messages in a bottle, or glimmers from the other side of the mirror.

There is little doubt that for Robert Graves, exile from his home in Deía during the period of the Spanish Civil War and World War Two was a far greater wrench than leaving England had ever been. As he writes in the autobiographical short story 'God Grant Your Honour Many Years':

Thus we became wretched refugees, and wretched refugees we continued to be for ten years more until the Civil War had been fought to a bloody close, until the World War had broken out and run its long miserable course, and until the Franco Government, disencumbered of its obligations to the Axis, had found it possible to sanction our return. Reader, never become a refugee, if you can possible avoid it, even for the sake of that eventual happy homecoming... [stay] where you are, kiss the rod and, if very hungry, eat grass or the bark off trees. To live in furnished rooms and travel about from country to country... homesick and disorientated, seeking rest but finding none, is the Devil's own fate.

But Graves' exile was, ultimately, a choice. The enforced exile of the refugee, the flight from terror and from war, the fear of armed men appearing in one's street with intent to harm or murder, is today a plight which, sadly, seems as inevitable as ever it was if you happen to live in Syria, or any one of a dozen other countries. However, I would like to focus on a very different part of the world: a zone that extends from Collioure in France down the coast to Portbou, just inside Spain, and inland a little to the village of Rabós, where I have lived on and off for twenty years, a region that the Catalan surrealist painter Joan Ponç referred to portentously as the 'ground zero of the universe'. The area is sometimes known as 'Greek Catalunya' and there is a topographical resemblance to the Greek landscape: sheer rockfaces, isolated headlands, an agriculture based on olives and vines, and from many vantage points a view of the sea.

Rabós is part of a landscape that might serve as a trope for transit; nestling beneath the Alberas, the range that falls towards the sea at the eastern end of the Pyrenees, it is surrounded on all sides by markers of the past, most notably dozens of Neolithic dolmens and burial chambers that are scattered over the ridges and hillsides, commanding views of the Bay of Roses to the east, the snow-covered peaks of Mount Canigó to the north-west, and the extensive plain of the Ampurdán, stretching towards Girona in the south. Hannibal passed this way with his elephants – elephant remains have been found nearby and dated to the second century BC – and the serial civil wars of Spain have made the place a crossing point in more recent centuries. Traffic has also come the other way, as we shall see. Travelling north out of Rabós, one can walk to France in an hour and a half; by car you can drive there in twenty minutes. The trail past the ninth-century monastery of Sant Quirze, which only became a covered road in the late 1990s, used to be known, in Catalan, as *el camí dels contrabandistes* – the smuggler's trail – and from Sant Quirze it snakes over the Col de Banyuls into France. The place resonates with the echo of night crossings, of rushed departures, of struggle and of loss.

This region was a focal point of movement in and out of Spain at the end of the Civil War and throughout the World War that followed. My account describes the experiences of three individuals, two of them well-known writers, the third an unknown teenage girl who simply happened to be in the wrong place at the wrong time.

Antonio Machado has long been one of my favourite poets, and the victim of some of my earliest efforts at translation – a mistake, since Machado is a poet fiendishly resistant to translation, as others have discovered. He left Spain in late January 1939. He had been an active participant in and spokesperson for the Republican cause and exile seemed the only sensible course of action. His elderly mother needed medical care that she was unable to receive in Spain, and Machado, along with mother and brother, José, headed for France; the ultimate destination was Paris.

The small group travelling with the poet had to leave most of their luggage when they abandoned the car in the bottleneck of escaping vehicles during a violent rainstorm at Portbou. They were refused food or even water in Cerbères by the French authorities because they could not pay. They made it along the coast as far as Collioure and, after receiving financial help from the Spanish novelist Corpus Barga, they stayed at the hotel Bougnol Quintana, now seemingly deserted, but adorned with a plaque that states, simply: 'Antonio Machado, poète espagnol, est mort dans cette maison le 22 février, 1939.'

Two years ago, after reading an article by Javier Cercas in *El País*, I visited Collioure to visit Machado's grave. I knew much of history already, but in Cercas' piece, he is given a strange account by two elderly English residents of Collioure, named the Weavers: according to them, Cercas tells us, in the days before the poet's death, Machado and José would never appear in the hotel dining room together, but always separately. Nobody could understand why this was, other than to put it down to some bad blood between the two, brought on by the hardships of exile. Only later was the truth discovered: they only had one suit between them and took it in turns to come down to eat. Antonio left the hotel only once, to visit the harbour, and sit for a while by the sea. He died three weeks after arriving in Collioure, victim to an undisclosed illness, probably pneumonia, although in popular legend he died of heartbreak at the fall of the Republic. His mother died three days later.

In the account given by Cercas, the story of Machado's last suit suggests that there are certain individuals who will not accept a loss of dignity even in the face of the worst of defeats, and that Spain will only have removed the last remaining anguish of its Civil War when, in Cercas' words, one is able to stand before Machado's grave without having to restrain one's tears for his sake, and on that day the war will truly be over.

Fifteen minutes down the coast from Collioure by car, Portbou lies just inside Spanish territory. I first walked this coastline on a baking June afternoon in 1984, arriving dehydrated and exhausted at the crossing, where the border guard, who was about to be relieved from his shift, took pity on me and suggested we adjourn to the adjacent bar for a beer. That night I slept on the beach. The border post no longer exists and the bar is boarded up. But I have always felt an attraction to this ugly, shy little town. Today it exudes a strange, sad energy – a place that, with the cessation of European frontiers, has lost its purpose as a centre for customs control. All that remains of its past glory is its vast and cavernous railway station.

Portbou was the final destination of the German philosopher and polymath, Walter Benjamin. On 25 September 1940, following seven years' exile in France and numerous changes of address, Benjamin, along with two other asylum-seekers, the photographer Henny Gurland and her son Joseph, was guided across the Alberas from Banyuls and arrived in Portbou. Benjamin, suffering from a heart condition, found the crossing extremely arduous. Nowadays, in a display of cultured tourist chic, there are signposts on the mountainside offering instructions on how to follow in his tracks: the Walter Benjamin Trail, which continues with key landmarks into Portbou itself, terminating at the spot where the hotel once stood in which he died (next door to the recently demolished Guardia Civil barracks). Benjamin carried a provisional American passport issued by the US Foreign Service in Marseilles, which was valid for land travel across Spain to Portugal, where he aimed to catch a ship to the USA. There, he hoped to join his friends Horkheimer and Adorno and resume the work of the Frankfurt School in America.

However, Benjamin was prevented entry to Spain because he had no French exit visa. Perhaps because of his evident ill-health, perhaps because of a border guard's Republican sympathies, his return to France was postponed until the next day and he was allowed to spend the night in a *pension*, the Hotel de Francia, rather than in police custody. The following day he was found dead in his room. He had taken an overdose of morphine.

According to a dedicated website on Walter Benjamin in Portbou, 'The Last Passage': 'If they [Benjamin and his companions] had arrived a day earlier, they would not have been refused entry to Spain: a change of orders had been received that very day. If they had arrived a day later, they would probably have been allowed in.' The Gurlands, at any rate, were permitted to continue their journey, and a few days later, Henny and Joseph boarded a ship for America. Benjamin, apparently, carried on him a small amount of money in dollars and francs, which were changed into pesetas to pay for the funeral four days later. In the judge's documentation the dead man's possessions are listed as 'a leather suitcase, a gold watch, a pipe, a passport issued in Marseilles by the American Foreign Service, six passport photos, an X-ray, a pair of spectacles, various magazines, a number of letters, and a few papers, contents unknown...', a tragic list that successfully conveys the essence of rushed and involuntary departure – exile, in a word.

After seven years of wandering, Benjamin's suicide in Portbou can been seen as an act of defiance against the Nazi terror by one of the most lucid thinkers of the modern era. However, no aspect of Benjamin's death is definitively closed. One hypothesis even holds that Benjamin was killed by Stalinist agents (the argument for this hypothesis is summarised by Stuart Jeffries in his *Observer* article 'Did Stalin's killers liquidate Walter Benjamin?'). In an intriguing turn, his guide across the mountains, Lisa Fittko, who died in 2005, referred on many occasions to 'the suitcase with a manuscript that Benjamin jealously guarded as a valuable treasure.' Was this a different suitcase from the one referred to in the judge's report? Unlikely, as the refugees were limited by their guide to one piece of luggage each. Were the 'few papers' referred to in the judge's report his final manuscript, or did this go missing? The authors of 'The Last Passage' seem not to know, and conclude that 'the suitcase was never found and its fate is unknown', which would contradict their earlier reference to the judge's report. However, another account, cited by Stuart Jefferies in his *Observer* article, records that Benjamin's briefcase, containing the elusive manuscript, was entrusted to an unnamed fellow refugee, who 'lost it on a train from Barcelona to Madrid'.

The extraordinary memorial *Passages* at Portbou was created by Israeli artist Dani Karavan, and sits next to the cemetery where Benjamin was buried. It comprises an enclosed staircase of eighty-seven rusty steel steps down which one can walk, terminating in a thick transparent glass wall that protrudes thirty metres above the blue waters of the bay. An inscription reads that 'it is more arduous to honour the memory of the nameless than that of the renowned. Historical construction is devoted to the memory of the nameless.' Puzzling, that last sentence, since history forgets the nameless masses, definitively. Perhaps the translation from the German is at fault. But the memorial itself is memorable.

My third account is more personal.

I was visiting a friend, Ramona, and her mother, Victoria, in Castelló d'Empúries, twenty minutes' drive from Rabós. I'd last seen Victoria at the funeral of Ramona's husband, Lluís Peñaranda, a Catalan artist with whom I had been friends since the mid-1980s. Victoria was ninety years of age, and the meeting took place in 2012, two years after Lluís' death. As though making an announcement, Victoria, who was delicate-boned and frail, but alert and inquisitive in her manner, said, 'I have a story for you, Richard'. I am transcribing this from notes that I took immediately afterwards.

In the final weeks of the Civil War, Rabós provided a staging post for the shattered remnants of the Republican army, and these stragglers were provided with food and shelter before crossing into France. The soldiers slept in the church, in the village hall, and in the narrow, cobbled streets. It was February, 1939, and the nights were cold. A soup kitchen was set up and Victoria, then aged seventeen, along with other volunteers, was able to provide a little nourishment to the exhausted men. The soldiers killed whatever mules remained for meat, hunted rabbits, and might, if they were lucky, shoot the occasional wild boar, though most of these had already been taken by hungry locals. The war was lost, and Victoria, in speaking of those days, evoked the utter devastation of this rag-tag army, but also, I noted, a sense of pride in her teenage self, an excitement at having been able to do something to help by working at the kitchen and caring for the soldiers, many of whom were wounded. Her father was a member of the Guardia Civil in nearby Figueres, and one of the few who had remained loyal to the Republic. Although she was able to cadge a lift home to her parents most nights, sometimes she had to sleep over in Rabós and it was on such a night that the news came through that a large detachment of enemy troops was on its way, and she became caught up in the mass exodus from the village without being able to get a message home. Perhaps she felt obliged to remain with the team of nurses tending to the wounded, or simply got caught up in the general panic, but one way or another she found herself a refugee in France, hoarded into the encampment at Argelès-sur-Mer. No one knew what was going to happen next, what was to become of them.

Rumours abounded and food was scarce. The French gendarmerie didn't seem particularly welcoming, that much was certain. However, she remained only two weeks in the makeshift camp at Argelès before being transported by train to a large camp near Clermont Ferrand, where the refugees were given basic accommodation and food. At this point, her story became rather vague; it seemed as though the passage of the years had transformed her memory of the camp at Clermont into an indeterminate blur of days and nights with no foreseeable conclusion. Many died of malnutrition and dysentery. But Victoria was a resourceful young woman and she got lucky. Among the refugees, she happened into a man, a member of the Guardia, who knew her father, and this man acted as some kind of go-between with the French authorities. Somehow – she was elusive as to the exact nature of its acquisition – she managed to secure a pass to travel by train to Biarritz, and from there crossed over into Irún, the frontier town close by San Sebastian. Six months had passed since her flight from Rabós, and she had not been able to get word to her family. She realised that they probably assumed she was dead. In San Sebastian, she knew no one, but was determined to get home. She begged from strangers, cajoled, insisted that she had to get back to Catalunya. 'You can't go there' one person told her, 'they [the fascists] are killing everyone'. But others were willing to help. Someone gave her money and she managed to board a train for Barcelona, and from there – because the rail tracks had been bombed by the Luftwaffe – a bus to Girona, and from there another to Figueres. At this point, she paused in her story, perhaps because its conclusion was so unlikely. 'When I stepped off the bus in the market place at Figueres the first person I saw was my mother.' Her father has been detained by the fascists in Girona prison, where he was tortured and would die shortly after his release. The news of her father's imprisonment soured her return, but the journey itself had been something of a miracle, a round trip of eight months, in which she had escaped, encountered the deprivations of two refugee camps, escaped again, and come back home across a war-torn country.

Victoria's story seems to me exemplary in so many ways: how the innocence of a teenager can unravel within the space of a few short months, how refugees were welcomed by the French authorities in 1939 and are treated still today across Europe, and the way – in spite of her given name – in which her round trip serves as a kind of elaborate trope for Spain's defeat. She arrived home an adult, her father imprisoned, the land laid waste, and her language forbidden.

Living again in an era of mass exodus and of refugees being turned away by unsympathetic governments, an era which the veteran war correspondent Patrick Cockburn described recently as one of War without End across an entire swathe of the planet – in which even the relative comforts of European unity are threatened by fragmentation thanks to the resurgence of nationalism and a political tunnel vision almost inconceivable to anyone with even the vaguest sense of history – makes the experiences of Machado, Benjamin and Victoria seem only too real. A border might be an idea wedded to a geography, but that idea has teeth and claws. If we take the memorial to Benjamin seriously, we must also take to heart the plight of those nameless hordes who each week become refugees, and whose nameless shadows we find mirrored in ourselves.

Ce qu'il reste à vivre

MARILYN HACKER

I waste the hours still left to me of life:
laundry, bronchitis, weightless messages,
perpetual distraction of the news:
disaster with explanatory graph,
a photo, survivors' shock and disbelief,
multiplied hourly in two languages.
I nurse my conscience, old child nursing a bruise.
Distress, desire, dismay, digression, grief
for the improbable. A passion turned
to an exchange of trivialities,
while crucial friendship dribbles out long distance.
A revolution where the cities burned
made the insurgents into refugees
and bare survival saps all their resistance.

And then it seemed survival meant resistance
to the unspeakable – its blusters, threats,
simian menaces and caprine bleats
(unfair to animals), sleepless insistence
that all remain aware of its existence...
The splattered incoherence of its tweets
has sullied discourse, silenced our regrets
with fear and loathing. Oh, remember Wystan's
late lively efforts at a tour de force,
inured to politics by words in orders,
echoing Middle English, Greek, Latin, Norse,
that he could, wistful, ludic, rearrange.
The monoglots are having their revenge,
armed at their checkpoints, shutting down borders.

Subletters, roommates, short-term tenants, boarders
in wintry walk-ups of precarity –
unemployed, overage, widowed, refugee
or redundant – senescent hoarders
of lit mags, Libyan dinars, rolls of quarters:
here we are, hunkered down, superfluous.
The times are dark. The dark settles on us.
Disaster's somewhere that they've sent reporters.
It's night at five again. The paisley throws
still rumpled in the morning's disarray,

would make a Flemish still-life. Write till nine,
but just translations, footnotes, throwaway
opinion, and, more lightly (I suppose)
another postcard about rain and wine.

Another postcard about rain and wine,
gracenote in a cacophony of wars,
posted, during a brief foray outdoors
in hovering daylight, in the rain again.
A year of our disgrace is closing down –
so many plurals might define that 'our.
'White women have a lot to answer for',
a friend wrote, smarting, who is neither one.
Ahed Tamimi, Palestinian
resistant, high-schooler, veteran at sixteen,
came at them bare-handed, *a pagan spear
invading* the invaders. Her wild hair
tied back, she looked, in the Israeli courtroom, 'white',
sat in an Israeli jail, last night, tonight.

بدون, you say it, waking in the night,
a heartbeat word, without, without, without
friendship love sunlight fortune freedom – doubt
a constant, like injustice. Down a flight
of stairs, the drilling starts at half-past eight,
while, on a screen, an article about
Ahed, her child face as the guard shoves her out
of range, her crinkled mane catching the light
– accompanied by words: eight months in jail
where she will study, study war some more.
She could be Rachel Corrie's younger sib.
She could be in Suweida or Idlib,
or coming upstairs with bread, milk, the mail,
taking her shoes off when she comes in the door

As he knelt in the doorway to take off his shoes,
we were already volleying conversation
about... for three years, it was 'revolution',
the last Skype, the next night flight, how to be of use,
and what – doctorate, girlfriend – he might lose

to all-night dispatches, three-way translation,
my jade buddha , his imposed vocation,
since he could…
                    An old and almost stateless Jew's
opinions braided with new verbs for
desire, dismay, a waft of cardamom,
when we'd gone upstairs with the dictionaries.
What's happened to the revolutionaries?
Silence. A conversation that's become
irrelevant, a footnote, an erasure.

Not even a footnote – an erasure
of her name from this memoir by her ex.

I put the book down. We each have our own facts.
Ivory/onyx votive figures, stature
ascending, fill a luminous enclosure ,
because her face, hieratic, was like that –
when she wasn't rolling a cigarette
as she scribbled and drank coffee, her composure
the tension of a dancer on a wire,
at once an artist and a prisoner,
extracting a poem from a news-brief
that in my own penumbra I'd translate,
while she, in her exile's elsewhere, stayed up late
devouring hours still left to her of life

Reading by the Light of a Black Sun

On Toby Martinez de las Rivas and Dave Coates

HENRY KING

BECAUSE ONE OF THE THINGS I admire about the reviews Dave Coates posts on his blog is how scrupulously he acknowledges his personal connections, let me start by explaining that I don't know him, but I do know Toby Martinez de las Rivas. Not intimately: we've never met, only exchanged a few emails; I approached him to write an essay for the centenary celebration of C. H. Sisson in *PNR* 217, and I chose to place his contribution first in that feature. So when Coates draws on that essay to attack Martinez de las Rivas ('On the Pale Sun of Toby Martinez de las Rivas', davepoems.wordpress.com, 13 September 2018), I have a stake in mounting a defence. But if that doesn't put me beyond the pale, I want to argue two things: firstly, that Coates is wrong about Martinez de las Rivas and *Black Sun* being fascist; secondly, and in a way more importantly, that Coates is wrong about *argument*. But before getting to the detail of Coates's attack, let's note some *prima facie* evidence. Back in 2009 when his Faber New Poets pamphlet came out, Martinez de las Rivas was described as living 'in Gateshead where he teaches English to asylum seekers and refugees'. A cunning disguise for a fascist intent on 'erasing the poor and outcast'! Coates seems unaware of, or simply ignores, such facts.

Coming to the essay, the problem is that Coates consistently reads into Martinez de las Rivas's words the most nefarious possible meanings. When Martinez de las Rivas states that the image of a black sun stands in one poem as 'a symbol of vengeance rising over London', Coates takes this as a plea for 'divine retribution against the country's biggest and most racially diverse city'. That's one possible interpretation, but there are other reasons to feel '[h]ostile to the metropolis': there is the Square Mile, the centre of a reckless financial culture that caused a recession and provided the pretext for a decade of austerity; luxury homes bought solely as invest-

ments, driving up property prices and rents beyond what working people can afford; the vanity of Boris Johnson's mayoralty; and the fact that London's air quality is so poor it broke the legal limit for the year one month into 2018. London, like a black sun, can stand for many things; hostility towards it doesn't necessarily mean hatred of other cultures and races.

Citing the interview again, Coates emphasises the comment that, 'Other poems are concerned with the larger body of the state, and the importance to me of the coherence of that body, so readers might detect positions that are, perhaps, monarchist, Unionist, and Anglican.' Apparently it's bizarre, 'given the anti-imperial, anti-establishment consistencies in Jesus of Nazareth's thinking, [that] Martinez de las Rivas draws a straight line between the physical body of the holy individual and the symbolic body of a national culture and State.' Coates may find it bizarre, but it's actually a longstanding tradition within Christian thought. Saint Paul writes that 'just as the body is one and has many members, and all the members of the body, though many, are one body, so it is with Christ. For by one Spirit we were all baptised into one body' (1 Corinthians 12:12–13). He was in turn borrowing from a common allegory of the state as a body, as in Menenius's speech to the citizens in *Coriolanus*: 'There was a time when all the body's members / Rebelled against the belly' (I.i.88–9). Saint Augustine synthesised these in his ideal City of God, which I take to be 'the State that is only / an image of the body inviolate, / the nation that extends through all time & space' – a spiritual 'nation' that *includes* England, but isn't identical with or reducible to it. So there is an intellectual tradition besides fascism for linking the individual body and the body politic – a conservative tradition, yes; but not all forms of conservatism are fascist.

As for concern with the coherence of that body, that too can mean different things. The Brexit vote revealed a form of incoherence that should concern people on both the left and the right: a polarised polity in which many cannot understand the other side except in apocalyptic terms, for instance as 'people who destroy a country because their passports aren't blue'. Coates's implication, there, that Martinez de las Rivas is an ardent Leave supporter is strange, given that in the *LARB* interview he explains how precarious Brexit has made his residence in Europe. Later, referring back to the passage from the interview, Coates says, 'I detect his monarchism, Unionism and Anglicanism quite distinctly... I have no reason to believe he has lied about all his other beliefs about the necessary purity of the body politic.' But Martinez de las Rivas did not say 'purity', he said 'coherence'; one term, with a range of meanings that includes a functional democracy, has been swapped out for another with more ominous implications. I don't think Coates has made this change in bad faith; no doubt he sees this as a decoding of what Martinez de las Rivas really means. But this kind of subtle rewording makes me uneasy.

My unease grows when Coates turns to the poetry. As I've said, I admire his reviews a great deal; he's normally an excellent critic. So I'm surprised that, to my ear, his readings here seem tone-deaf. In 'At Lullington Church: To My Daughter', Coates hears a 'ham-fisted reference to the historical falconry of Yeats's "The Second Coming", another poem written by a high church Protestant with dreams of pure nationhood ruled by aristocracy, who also gravely feared the unclean, unholy masses "slouching toward Bethlehem".' Maybe; but Coates misses or ignores allusions to the medieval Corpus Christi Carol, in which 'the falcon has borne my mate away'. Martinez de las Rivas goes to such lengths to make this allusion plain that he mars the sonnet form by tagging on the Carol's ululating refrain, '*Lully, Lulley, Lully, Lulley*', brought to mind by the similarity to Lullington. Medievalism is conservative in some senses, but not necessarily fascistic. Near the end of his album *Grace*, Jeff Buckley segues from the Carol into the noisy anti-racist song 'Eternal Life'. William Morris was a socialist who loved medieval art and the English countryside. Allusions to falconry don't spell the 'dream of a white nation' unless one reads that in.

These are small but cumulative points about interpretation; I want to turn now to argumentation, and Martinez de las Rivas's essay on Clemo and Sisson. Coates quotes the first sentence:

> In the last few years, 'radical' as an epithet in poetry has come to be shorthand for a very particular kind of writing: politically submissive to Marxist dogma, syntactically committed to what is now termed the 'interrupted lyric', historically associated in the UK with the Cambridge School, and metaphysically derived from a range of post-structuralist continental thinkers.

Coates claims that this lacks a 'solid referent' (as if language works as simply as that!) and any account of the following issues:

> who uses 'radical' in this way, who is writing this kind of poetry, what evidence he has that they are Marxist, what being

'politically submissive' to Marxism means in practice, which Marxist 'dogma' in particular they are submissive to, what it means to be 'syntactically committed' to anything, who has used the term 'interrupted lyric' and about whom...

The full list of questions goes on for almost the same length again; the answers – which could be adduced – would add up to a monograph. Coates's main complaint, though, is that 'you, and most certainly subscribers to *PN Review*, probably know exactly who he's talking about', and that '[w]hile I sit here puzzling through his word salad, he and those sympathic [sic] to his airy generalities have already won'. Basically, that Martinez de las Rivas is using rhetorical skulduggery.

Was Martinez de las Rivas underhand in not giving us the book-length account of the avant-garde Coates desires? Was I, as his editor, remiss in not putting to him similar questions? I think not. He was doing what people always do: arguing from premises the audience will, at least provisionally, agree with. Aristotle called this the enthymeme, and made it central to his theory of rhetoric (used nonpejoratively). When I say that people always do this, I include myself and Coates, as when he jokes, 'I keenly await critiques from those conservative critics who complain of there being excessive "politics" in the poetry of marginalised authors denouncing Martinez de las Rivas' explicitly ideological agenda.' No names need be named; the gesture is enough because his readers 'probably know exactly who he's talking about'. Let me be clear: I am not saying this is illegitimate; it is the normal way of working with one's audience. But as a consequence, I think it's wrong to find evidence there of bad faith and the naked will to power. Coates may find Martinez de las Rivas' argumentation 'wild', but it strikes me as no less wild than his identification of 'a committed neo-Georgian ruralism' with outright fascism.

I'll grant Coates a point when he asks of Martinez de las Rivas, 'if desiring right-wing politics in art is an unbreakable taboo, how did you just break it?' The tactic is weak because it withstands so little scrutiny. But I find it less worrisome than Coates's closing gambit. He concludes, 'There will almost certainly be people who read this essay and see nothing but conspiracy theory and speculation, rather than a series of red flags, the visible residue of a totalising ideology. That is fine. If that is where you are right now, I was never going to convince you.' In a nutshell, this means 'if you don't agree with me, you are already beyond redemption'. For all his appeals to 'messiness and compromise', this manoeuvre is itself totalising: it excludes the possibility of reasoned, respectful disagreement, which democracy relies on and which I've tried to articulate. (I'm not claiming left-wing ideology is 'totalising' in the sense he means it, or that socialists are the real Nazis; I'm saying that, just there, Coates betrays himself into totalising rhetoric.)

Martinez de las Rivas clearly has some conservative tendencies, and I don't question Coates's right to criticise that ideology – in fact I applaud the work he's done, for instance, in highlighting the imbalance of representation in poetry reviewing. But he has not convinced me that Martinez de las Rivas is a fascist whose 'vision would necessarily entail... cultural cleansing, mass deportation, [and] genocide', and it doesn't serve democracy, or poetry, to paint him as one.

Three Poems

JAMES RICHARDS

Damascus Public Library

For Ahmad

We search in the rubble for
books.
　　　When we find them, we leave
a note that tells the owner
where to collect them if they
come back.
　　　　　People loan the books
they like. The women don't go
outside because of the bombs
so they ask the children and
the men to get books for them.

We get many requests for
*Seven Habits of Highly
Effective People, The Art
of Dealing With People* and
The Alchemist.
　　　　　Shockwaves caused
by the bombs knock books off the
shelves and cover everything
with white dust.

　　　　　There is no food
here. A lot of time happens
and there is nothing to do.
Our best friends in this city
are books.
　　　　When we see a child
who wants to eat a tiny
piece of bread or hopes to watch
TV to feel happy, or
a young girl who is crying
because her father has died,
or bodies spread over the
street, it affects us.
　　　　　The books
give us hope that there is light
at the end of the tunnel.

Tibet

The windows are on fire
this January night

as the blizzard lays
its language along the slope.

This is not unlike Tibet
I say out loud

not unlike Tibet
　　　　not unlike...

You were asleep there too,
the batteries shelled

from the alarm clock,
sweet incense.

Here, something grows
in the shadow of the bed.

In your dream you swipe at it
and the prayer wheels come back

come back
　　　come back to me

Cultural Exchange

I intend to go to Seville,
get drunk on wine, assiduously,
eat a part of a pig's anatomy
and walk the lamplit streets
becoming sick, sick with love,
sick with sick, sicking up
an intact postcard of Andover,
of Exeter, of Whitechapel.

Dementia and other poems

NINA BOGIN

Dementia

Has seized our marriage by the throat.
Made us snap and snarl and spit.
Slap. Shout. Hit.

Heart pounds. Door bangs.
Pace outside, let it settle.
It's summer, it's beautiful.

I pout, sulk.
Shrug. Sigh. Frown.
Who is this woman I've become?

The girl you married with long black hair.
Your honey-brown eyes, your voice, so warm.
Your trust. Mine.

It was good for a long time.
Now your gaze is veiled,
you wear someone else's smile.

Your voice wobbles,
anxious, edgy.
You're fidgety, crotchety.

Where's my flashlight,
my shoe horn, my book?
Where did you put

my cell phone, my glasses?
And now I've lost my *carte vitale*,
my *carte d'identité*!

Yes, husband, your identity
has been misplaced,
mishandled, misshapen,

slowly crumbling
like your old ski boots
we found years later

that fell apart in our hands
in an avalanche
of powder.

K.

What comes next?
And after that? And then?
No set path, no

familiar cobblestones
or open doorways,
none. Doors

locked, windows shuttered.
Weren't they always?
The little house

with the blue shutters
I dreamed myself into –
an illusion. I see myself

in a tiny kitchen as through
the wrong end
of a pair of binoculars.

Where shall we go?
And how shall we get there?
Our future, yours and mine,

disappears around the bend.
Like K.
in the snowbound village,

striving to reach the castle.
Land surveyor who could not
gauge the land, shuttled

from one inn to another,
at last he descended
to the rooms of the barmaids

in the depths of yet another labyrinth,
suspended at the end
of an unfinished chapter.

Hallowe'en

Little girl lavender, little boy blue,
here's a pumpkin split in two,

on each side half a grin
with some teeth out and some teeth in,

a triangle nose and two wide eyes
that wink at you, that wink at you.

Here are two candles for you to light,
one for each half of a Hallowe'en night

when long-toothed shadows
flicker high and burn down low

in pumpkins that keep watch until
morning comes to windowsills.

We can't stick the two halves back
together, can't fix the marriage pact

when it goes against the grain.
What once was, can't be again –

a lesson
it takes a lifetime to learn.

Warm beneath your eiderdowns
you'll sleep through the night of Hallowe'en

in this house or the other,
with your father or mother

and a harvest moon –
only one –

over the park, over the patio.
Be at peace, and know

that a parent's love cannot be halved
but rather doubled, multiplied –

so unwavering are
the ties of the heart.

As October steals into November,
here are words for you to remember,

little boy blue, little girl lavender.

Slippers

I rue the day
I bought you those

black leather mules
you clump around the house in

and won't abandon
at any price

though they slow you down
to an old man's

shuffle
you seem almost thankful

to adopt.
I guess

each slipper is a place
your foot

feels at home in –
unlike shoes

that are hard to put on
and shoelaces

you can no longer tie,
when at my request

you trail along behind me,
you who walked so fast,

on errands that take us
into this shop or that

when you'd rather be back
in the comfort

of your armchair.
That must be why

you tote your mules
on every outing

even if they stay
in the car,

while your life
gets smaller

and more confined
as it fits around

an ever-diminishing
version of you,

your world in a shoe,
your home in a slipper,

your bed snug
as a hand-knit sock.

Spice Cupboard

Juniper and clove,
thyme and tarragon.
Who can I depend upon?

Star anise and linden flower,
I went away, and even further.
I broke the hearts of my father and mother.

Rosemary and marjoram.
I married, we had a son
who stayed in the womb,

who wasn't born.
Sorrow of lemon balm.
Solace of hypericum.

Lavender and coriander.
We had a daughter
and another daughter.

Raspberry leaf, chamomile and cinnamon.
My first daughter has a daughter
and a son.

Cardamom and ginger root,
cumin and turmeric.
This is my second daughter's music.

Poppy seed and elderflower.
I'm not yet old,
but getting older.

Gingko, saffron and dill
will not cure
my husband's ills.

Marigold and rue,
hyssop and shepherd's wort.
All I haven't learnt.

Bay leaf, sage and caraway.
Which confers wisdom?
Which longevity?

Nasturtium and rose,
starflower and clover.
Flowers to think things over.

Anthony Rudolf's *Silent Conversations*

FREDERIC RAPHAEL

I FIRST, AND LAST, read Elias Canetti's 1935 novel, *Die Blendung,* under its English title, *Auto-da-fe*, in the early 1950s in Cambridge. My adhesive memory is of a man whose living space is voluminously pre-empted by print. Dr Peter Kien adheres to an obsessive version of Logan Pearsall Smith's dictum, 'People say that life's the thing, but I prefer reading'. Kien's housekeeper Therese is seemingly the dedicated guardian of his library, the biggest in bookish Vienna; but when the bibliomaniac marries her, she becomes a termagant who eventually deprives him of contact with his one true love.

Since the principal victims of the original Inquisition's *auto-da-fe* were Jews, it calls for no great wit to see Kien's fate as emblematic of the impending destiny of the People of the Book whom 'Aryan' racial vanity – the inferiority complex in Boss uniform – would eliminate from the central European scene which they had done so much to enlighten. Canetti was the augur of the imminent collapse of the delusion that literacy is a reliable barrier against barbarism (music, as Wagner proved, makes no such promises). Nazi 'philosophers' and Stalinist ideologists soon established that addled reason and parodic scholarship could supply a warrant for mass murder. Straight philosophers, Kant and Schopenhauer among them, had already flirted with the systematic anti-Semitism which most German historians, Theodor Mommsen not least, repudiated. Karl Marx proved his emancipation from antique loyalties by a show of detached disgust with 'the huckster race'.

Socialist anti-Semitism derives from these lethal schematics. Does Reason, with its logical discounting of the first personal (aka 'mere autobiography'), dispose philosophers, and their political followers, to become callous as well as categorical? Aristotle set the style by telling Alexander the Great that the Persians were barbarians, hence not entitled to humane consideration; cf. the Crusaders with Muslims and Jews, Hitler with 'Slavs', after breaking his pledge to Stalin when the two of them tore Poland in half along the dotted line.

Anthony Rudolf's *Silent Conversations* has been largely ignored by the literary intelligentsia. It is tempting to attribute this to malice; laziness is more plausible. The book is fat and, if leavened with nice touches of self-deprecation, compiled with sustained *sérieux*. One has the impression, not infrequently, that Rudolf could express himself more happily in French. The introduction might have been designed to warn off what Wittgenstein called 'tourists':

> My book, like many literary works, involves excess, desire and the controlling hand of absolute possession, certainly where reading and re-reading are concerned. Subject matter and form are dialectically interrelated, and out of the interrelationship is born the book's deep content, which is the love child of conscious and unconscious longings for healing and wholeness, for unity and redemption... When I was a child, reading either completed the world or, better yet, *was* the world.

Shades of the Yeshiva enclose the growing boy, not least when hell has prefaced his infancy. Rudolf, whose grandparents came from Galicia, adjoining Ukraine, was born in London in 1942, the year of the Wansee Conference at which Heydrich and his staff, Adolf Eichmann among them, drafted the business-plan to murder Europe's Jews and (appetising supplementary ambition) appropriate their goods. Sigmund Freud had consoled himself, in 1938, that the Nazis burned books, not people; he died before mass incineration of human beings became typical of the last Inquisition ('the last' here signifies most recent, not ultimate).

Rudolf's fortunate place of birth did not determine his consciousness nor – despite a middle-class education, culminating at Cambridge – give him the notion, common among British Jews, that he belonged, culturally, to the Anglo-Saxon world. If he has literary cousins, Walter Benjamin, that thoughtful collagist – whom Rudolf declares to have been 'intoxicated by anamnesis' – is probably the closest. Intoxication can stand for a kind of ecstasy and also, etymologically, for taking poison, as Benjamin did in Portbou in 1940.

The man who remembers everything lives in an embottled world. To be totally unforgetting entails having no mental space/time for the present. In Rudolf's case, a long habit of campaigning for good causes, Nuclear Disarmament the keenest, has taken him away from his shelves and involved him in the world of *bien-pensant* conferences and colloquies and, during a forty-year career, of publishing an unashamedly elitist, cosmopolitan list, often of poets, Yves Bonnefoy *en tête*. Throughout Rudolf's *catalogue raisonné* of his accumulated books, there is a refusal, if not an inability, to salt or sugar it with complacency of the kind that made *Scrutiny* the bastion of unsmiling priggishness, Kingsley Amis the standard-bearer of the cheers-then school of aggressive light-heartedness – insularity their common badge.

Rudolf's Galician origins give him something in common with Joseph Roth (bifocal sharpness) as well as with his second cousin twice removed Jerzyk who killed himself, at the age of eleven, by swallowing cyanide. The boy's family was in hiding and, having been issued with poison pellets by his doctor father against the day of deportation, he presumed that the Gestapo had come to take them away. In fact, the thump on the door came from opportunist blackmailers, on the make for pay-offs. Jerzyk was to be the only child suicide in the records of Yad Vashem. His conscience-stricken parents survived the *Shoah,* had a daughter and went to live in Israel.

Rudolf's *Jerzyk* is a tribute to the dead boy and also a way of picking up the baton in the relay of Jewish life.

Although its author has some Hebrew, the religious tenets of Judaism, while observed in ritual respects, seem to matter little to him, as to the majority of western European (and American) Jews. The current cant likes to suggest, if not insist, that Jews in England have 'leaders', to whom ideologues such as Jeremy Corbyn apologise, *du bout de lévres*, as if to the chieftains of some essentially alien tribe. For the intellectually limited, ideology supplies potted education, answers at the back. In fact, whatever their vestigial allegiances and observations, most British Jews have more Anglican culture and social habits than Hebraic piety. H. G. Wells once said, 'Grown men don't need leaders'.

The split personality of Christian/secular Europe has the disputatious ingenuity of the Talmud at its hinge. That many copies were burnt in Paris by St Louis, in the thirteenth century, testifies to the Church's deep-rooted dread of alternative intelligence, Jewish in particular. But remember Abelard! Rudolf's reverence for literature and its producers (he has known more 'foreign' writers personally than I have heard of) is a function both of his English education and of his quick sense of its limitations. Despite a manifestly precocious intelligence, he acquired the distinction of failing his Tripos at Cambridge, an achievement matched, *mutatis mutandis,* by A. E. Housman at Oxford. If never a professor, Rudolf has since done his share of academic teaching; his publishing house, the Menard Press (mark the Borgesian conceit), which ran on an exiguous budget, resembled an outsider's All Souls' college with its own demanding, polyglot curriculum.

The post-Enlightenment Jewish personality reveals itself in an urgent desire to set or sustain durable values in art and, incidentally, in life; hence Wittgenstein's 'Hebraic' equation – in the *Tractatus* – of ethics and aesthetics. Logical positivism's dismissal of both in favour of a level intellectual playing field of mathematical and scientific truths was an attempt, in the 1920s and '30s, by a conclave of Viennese Jews and Gentiles, to substitute Science for Belief and its aggressive partialities. Whatever could not be proved or verified was adjudged – to use the young A. J. Ayer's term – 'literal non/sense'. Perhaps inadvertently, the Vienna Circle proposed to re-enact Plato's banishing of poets from the articulation of society.

No such scheme could be less to Rudolf's taste. His conviction that literature matters has no use for the popu/lit hedonism which denies the validity of aesthetic characteristics other than pleasure. Such a doctrine leaves even the smartest critic as no better than the presiding taster of the consumers' fun diet. John Carey's claim for attention, however backed by professorial credentials, depends less on his undoubted exegetical erudition than on the pimp's promise to show you a good time.

Untempted by larkiness, devoid of malice, Rudolf presumes that we will not chide or mock him for the solemnity of his eclecticism. A writer who coins the term 'endotic' to describe the anthropological distinction of Georges Perec's contribution to literature can have no fear of the loutish scorn of *Private Eye*, that smug coop of smart-alecry. The OED does list 'endote' as the obsolete verb used by Tyndall to describe the 'sacrifice' of their hair typical of friars at their initiation. Now a grandfather, Rudolf parades no affectations of sanctity, but his devotion to literature (especially to other people's) has been,

he says, 'one long fugue' from 'the responsibility I lay claim to – being a writer'.

His several books are mostly self-effacingly (and all but officiously) at the service of others' lives and visions; his keen verses are exercises in lyrical minimalism, akin to that of his admired George Oppen, whose heuristic communism – Walter Benjamin's term (in a letter to Gershom Scholem) for his own qualified allegiance to a cause which admits of no qualifications – finds an echo in Rudolf's unideological socialism as a panacea for the imminent catastrophes of nuclear annihilation and/or climate change.

The passionate charity with which he advocates schemes of human redemption is, to my mind, both noble and, alas indeed, impractical. The belief that the fractious selfishness of human beings, and their short-term appetites and hopes, can be hectored into common, long-term rectitude is as optimistic as, I fear, it is futile. When has the world had a more dismaying collection of second- and third-rate governors, of one kind and another? In the 1930s, Bertrand Russell proposed, as a cure for the irrational ravings of tyrants, that they be more reasonable. Today's leaders can rarely rise even to hypocrisy. The music goes round and round. Rudolf's high-mindedness, literally appealing as it is, seems to be a part of his 'fugue' rather than any kind of reliable anchorage. He cites Bonnefoy's admiration for Alfred de Vigny's reverence for 'the majesty of human suffering'. Is there something not entirely trustworthy, an element of envy perhaps, in that kind of sado-masochistic voyeurism? I recall Gabriel Fielding, the pseudonymous Roman Catholic author of *The Birthday King*, telling me, in 1963, 'I *love* Jews'. The grasping tone sounded like an invitation to run for one's life.

Marguerite Duras, an early (sequentially speaking) object of Rudolf's admiration, is cited as claiming that Joan of Arc had 'a political mind equal to Saint-Just, a judgment which would have astonished Luis Buñuel but not Carl Dreyer'. Colour me baffled; Dreyer's film, although based on records of Jeanne's trial, was silent, Saint-Just *non plus.* Bernard Shaw is unmentioned in a context which might have been enlightened, in this instance at least, by his opinionated verbosity. Would anyone of civilised temper care to live in a kingdom under the regency of Jeanne d'Arc's patriotic Christianity?

As for Duras, her famous qualities need not be doubted (François Mitterrand's lover, she won the *Prix Goncourt* in 1984), but my clippings-laden memory recalls that she wrote a pamphlet denouncing the mother of '*le petit Grégory*', a four-year-old found murdered in the department of the Vosges in the early 1980s. Duras's authority as a star of the Resistance, lent cruel credibility to an accusation belatedly recognised as without foundation. Grégory's mother was proved innocent; the *juge d'instruction*, whose early intimate conviction primed the assumption of her guilt, committed suicide. Did Duras ever think better of her opportunistic insolence?

Her husband, retrieved from Dachau in 1945, weighing under forty kilos, by Mitterrand, was Robert Antelme, whose *The Human Race* Rudolf claims to be 'as valuable as Primo [Levi]'s *If This Be A Man*'. I confess that I had never heard of it. Rudolf, fluent in French, scarcely mentions Sartre but puts a gentle boot into Albert Camus:

'had he lived into old age... I suspect that Camus would have sounded like a mild version of Emil Cioran, that arch pessimist and cynic. Politically, I wonder where Camus and, say, George Orwell would stand re, say, Iraq.'

Is this implicit denunciation convincing? I am in the middle of reading Camus's fat *Correspondance* with Maria Casarès, which begins in the late 1940s. It is revealing of the Nobel prizeman's fragility and his all but panicky need for love; but there is no trace of the seeds of cynicism in common with that of the misanthropic (self-hating?) Cioran. The latter's fascist past in Roumania led him, like Mircea Eliade, to reupholster himself, after the war, cf. Paul de Man. Cioran then donned the lineaments of Larochefoucauld's seventeenth-century prose; his latter-day piss-elegant pessimism also had something of Joseph Joubert's brevity but lacked any trace of the Perigordine generosity of spirit, without which, as Joubert remarked, criticism becomes spleen.

Rudolf implies that Camus and Orwell would have/ might have been on the 'wrong' side when it came to the invasion of Iraq in 2003 (never mind, I assume, the earlier 'correction' of Saddam Hussein, after he invaded Kuwait). A lot of us made the mistake of believing the 'evidence', adduced in the Commons, that Saddam possessed undestroyed chemical war-heads and harboured imminent malign purposes. If that had been true, would it have been wrong to deprive him of his weapons? If yes and no, as so often, what 'political' scale might afford us the proper reading?

Orwell's anti-communism, which, it has recently been disclosed, comprised an allegedly sneaky connection with MI5, has in some people's eyes marred that plain-speaker's reputation. There is small evidence indeed that either Orwell or Camus, enfeebled as both may seem by an inclination to consider both sides of an argument, would have fallen in with the crusading spirit of G. W. Bush and Tony Blair. More pertinently, Rudolf also cites Orwell's ominous prediction: 'if we fail to bring a European union into being, we shall be obliged, in the long run, to subordinate our policy to that of one Great Power or the other [...] and everyone knows [...] that we should choose America'. This has not inhibited J.C., in a recent *TLS*, from proclaiming that Orwell would have been a Brexiteer; in the current state of Great Britain, anything will do to fill a column.

Lurching pragmatism has yielded to shameless partisanship and exclusive vanity, including the local Leninism which has something, and we know what, in common with National Socialism. French and German languages, for key example, are of dwindling interest in English universities. Rudolf's vision of humanity locked in peace-loving, environment-conserving singlemindedness comes close to a project for a monoglot, all on the same floor, Babel which we all know to be impossible. 'Linguistic colonialism' will be the first complaint of those homogenised for the common good. How then shall we be saved? No mention is to be found, I think, in this copious volume, of Friedrich Hayek, Karl Popper or René Girard, all of whom, in differing ways, suggest a 'logic' more meliorist than apocalyptic, hence more plausible, if less enchanting.

In his personal life Rudolf is both principled and unpretentious. His self-deprecation – he accuses himself of 'cowardice in personal relations' – is the most British thing about him. Less insular is the scribble, scribble, scribble injunction to himself: 'I knew I must have a life on the page, because the page is where the forms of life speak to us most deeply'. The sentiment implies a scribe's affinity with George Steiner who regards Israel as the enemy of what is most precious in the Jew: a gift for what D. H. Lawrence called 'disinterested speculation'.

Michel Deguy is accordingly cited as saying, 'the greatest indictment of the Nazi war against the Jews is that it was a crime against humanity even more than... a specific genocide'. *Vous croyez?* The specificity is central to the logic of Christian and post-Christian Europe. Trotsky is quoted as saying, in 1938, 'it is possible to imagine without difficulty what awaits Jews at the mere outbreak of the future world war. But even without war, the next development of world reaction signifies with certainty the physical extermination of the Jews' – accurate and specific.

Hitler's accusation that the Jews were responsible for the unmanning invention of conscience – circumcision its objective correlative – is crucial to the fancy of their extinction and the substitution of national conceit for pan-European culture. Serious pessimists will have noted that even the nice Mrs May referred, with sinister innocence, to 'cosmopolitans' as the enemies of Brexit (Paris was worth a Mass to Henry of Navarre – Downing Street a similar conversion for a lady who proved more than willing to turn, if not wriggle). The central marginality of Jews continues to embarrass both the Left and meta-racist ideologues. Rudolf applauds the humanity of Rabbi Abraham Heschel who can be seen, in a famous photograph, marching side by side with Martin Luther King in Alabama in 1965. The 2014 film *Selma* excises him from the going record.

That intellectuals have some proper, hegemonic place in 'progressive' political movements is integral to their self-esteem. Geoffrey Hill is cited as saying 'difficult poetry is the most democratic because you are doing your audience the honour of supposing that they are intelligent beings'. Rudolf comments 'Amen to that'. I fear 'If only' is more like it. Hill's use of 'democratic' is like the young's use of 'amazing', a term with no more significant content than the implicit applause in one of J. L. Austin's 'performatives'. In brute fact, the Brexit referendum was both undoubtedly democratic and proved that simple, allegedly conclusive, majorities are the means of choice of the simple-minded and their manipulators. The notion that poets have legislative force has Shelleyan backing but small evidence in the statute book.

Poetry and poets receive dedicated attention here (nice to be told that Cid Corman ran an ice-cream parlour in Kyoto). Rudolf's embrace does not flinch from Ezra Pound, whose early *Near Perigord* is properly lauded, never mind its almost giggling allegation of Jews as usurers. Testing the waters is an aspect of Corbyn and his friends' recourse to anti-Semitism. Imagine if Mr Eliot had had the decency to tell Pound what Churchill declared to Hitler in the early 1930s: 'anti-Semitism is a good starter, but a bad sticker'. Then again, imagine if he'd thought it. Ol' Ez says some good things in Rudolf's unprejudiced register: 'The perception of the intellect is given in the word, that of the emotions in the cadence'; and then again:

'Most writers fail from lack of character rather than lack of intelligence'. Two ticks in the margin there, blast it.

Rudolf has few moments of impatience with the denizens of literature, but he loses it with regard to Olivia Manning's 'flow of insults at Sam Beckett'; they are deemed to be all you need to know about her. *La Manning* was tactless and self-advertising, but her trilogy *The Fortunes of War* is, as they will say, arguably superior to *Malloy* and, incidentally, to Evelyn Waugh's Crouchback number. Rudolf prefers Anthony Powell to Waugh in general. Tell you what, I prefer Sinclair Lewis to either.

The British have often distrusted those fluent in foreign languages (one of the reasons why Jews were often regarded as unreliable was their Janus-like role as interpreters). Rudolf has been at home with Russian, as well as French and other languages, and so is unblinkered when it comes to the curious discontinuity between the language, and its peerless qualities (noted by Turgenev and repeated, without attribution, by Nabokov), and the practices of those who speak it. Vasily Grossman, whose *Life and Fate* rivals *War and Peace,* is quoted as saying, 'When will Russia be free? Perhaps never'. This echoed Fyodor Tyutchev's earlier, woeful 'in Russia one must only believe'; Putin's coda: Or Else.

Rudolf nominates Gorbachev as 'the man of the twentieth century, as against Nelson Mandela, because the former "managed *perestroika...* without nuclear war"'. This is a nice but dubious claim to historical greatness, not least because *perestroika* was a brand name, without issue. Ilya Ehrenberg is also applauded, for saying 'you cannot deceive in art'. That ranks with Jean-Luc Godard's 'cinema is truth at twenty-four frames a second' as a statement which requires negation in order to have any instructive force (see above, re *Selma*). One has only to think of Paolo Veronese's *trompe-l'oeil* self-portrait, coming through a door in the mural in Palladio's Villa Maser, in the Veneto, as emblematic of the straight-faced trickery which spices representation. Nice that *ars est celare artem* is itself a fabricated quotation from Ovid.

Rudolf establishes, with a clarity that need not embarrass him any more than it forbids friendship, how the keenest readers can take partial views of the same author. Leo Rosten's *The Joys of Yiddish* may be properly praised, but there is no mention of the same author's *The Education of Hyman Kaplan,* one of the funniest books I have ever wept over. Who cannot smile at Hyman's hopeful classroom rubric 'mistakes by Mitnik'? There speaks the next generation's literary critic, avid to list contemporaries' faults, shambling towards *Dissent* to be boring.

Who can claim to be exempt from the '*oui, mais...*' tendencies of the literary fraternity? James Kennaway is applauded for saying 'No one is born an artist [...] concentration and selfishness [...] I have watched it in every living artist I know.' Generalisation can chime nicely with self-service. My daughter Sarah was indeed born an artist and, however hard she concentrated (no one harder), she was often unselfish, not least with regard to other painters.

Nietzsche, rightly saluted in these pages, spoke for civilisation when he remarked, 'You say there can be no argument about matters of taste? All life is an argument about matters of taste.' That I differ from Rudolf in many such matters (for instance, the 'beguiling' opening paragraph of Anthony Burgess's *Earthly Powers,* which – to my mind – promises, and delivers, a protracted exercise in heterosexual camp) does not entail disrespect for his evangelical literacy. The United States of the 1930s and the Spain of the *Convivencia* are to me what vanished Austria-Hungary is for Rudolf 'in some ways my homeland'. He revels in the lost world of Lou-Andréas Salome, Rainer Maria Rilke *et toute cette galère.* Their introspective life of lofty earnestness, self-absorption and self-advancement are the fallen leaves of the culture of *Mitteleuropa* which made Adolf Hitler and who all else feel inferior.

Rudolf's Viennese pen/chant extends to psychoanalysis. Jung is applauded for, 'Nothing exerts a stronger psychic effect upon the human environment, and especially upon children, than the life which the parents have not led'. This, to my mind, is a jewel of the higher bullshit. The word 'upon' is in general a marker for pretentiousness, 'once upon a time' excepted. Psycho-theory is seen as the scaffolding ('falsework' is the apt technical term) for understanding the human condition. Jean-Bertrand Pontalis, a psychoanalyst pupil of Jean-Paul Sartre, wins a place for, 'every language, beginning with the mother tongue, is a false language'. This is the antique Cretan paradox repackaged for the Smart-Ass Award: if it's true, it must be false, since it is expressed in language.

Who can finish *Silent Conversations* without wishing to join, vocally, in the proceedings, if only to query some of its humane presumptions? Its underlying (and, it would be nice to think, unquestionable) assumption is the feasibility of what the British used to call decency, a game played on common ground. Who will not fall silent when he scans the poem, on page 577, left behind by a nine-year-old victim of what the shameless deny ever took place, the Holocaust to which the fastidious Christopher Ricks refused a capital letter?

Once there was a girl Elzunia,
She's dying all alone now
Her daddy, he's in Majdanek,
Mummy in Auschwitz-Birkenau.
 (C/ Volatic Ltd, 2018).

Waiting for My Life to Begin and other poems

LAURA SCOTT

In which she learns the lost children are never found, only remembered.

It starts, it always starts, with her
watching them and everything else blurring around them

as they burst through the water's skin (again and again)
the years running off their limbs

the water washing them
back to what they were when she could still balance the weight

of each of them in turn on her left hip. That's how it starts.
The next move is when she tries to blink the sight of them

on to the back of her mind's eye so she can pull them out like a photo
from a drawer

but her eyes water and cloud –
so she tries something else:

to throw words around them like towels,
to pause the great gush of life of them into an aria

she can sing (again and again)

but the sun is so hot and anyway they're doing something else now.
It's nearly over when she gives up, she forgets

everything and her eyes clear.

But then the swallows come clipping and dipping the pool with their wings and beaks.

Try again say the swallows
but what do they know of time?

Waiting for my life to begin

I saw them skim the fence of your teeth
and slide out into the room. And I envied you,

oh how I envied you with all the four chambers of my heart –
to be bored like that, bored like an aristocrat

lying on a sofa somewhere in a room where the windows
stretch all the way down to the floor and the walls are blue

as the eyes of peacock feathers. *Waiting for my life to begin*

that's what you said, under your breath maybe
but you said it, in those words, those very words.

The mother and the son

They're on a train and he's taller than her now but his hair is still
a bit like hers, especially at the ends where it flicks out around his ears

and she likes that, really likes that – that they have the same hair –
and she's taking him – no she's not taking him, they're going together –

to the crossroads where she'll leave him. All she has to do is follow
the tracks cut deep into the ground like scars left by those who've been here

before. Sometimes, she sees faces pressing against the window, or looking up
at their carriage as it flies past. She thinks they were there, watching her

when she first brought him home, murmuring to each other as they moved in
closer to catch the smell of him as he lay in her arms. And now

they're telling her to leave him – *no* – they mouth at her through the window,
don't watch him, you mustn't do that, turn away so you don't see him step down

and walk away into the sea of people. But the thing is he's like a present, the best present
she has ever had, and they know that, and still they tell her to walk away,

so she does.

your eyes

If someone were to ask what colour
they are I wouldn't say

anything, anything at all. I'd sit there
silent as a spy before I'd turned

to look out of the window,
maybe I'd light a cigarette

and by the time the smoke escaped
from the side of my mouth

they'd forget they ever asked.
But if someone were to ask

what they're like I'd tell them
everything. I'd sing your eyes

like a canary. I'd tell them
they're hooded like a bird of prey's,

how they never blinked
how they waited and waited

for me to break cover
and how nearly I did.

I'd tell how they pulled me taut
for you and caught for you,

and how even now the slip
of a thought of them makes me

long for you, takes me back
through a door to you.

Water Music

STANLEY MOSS

David told me that years ago I said:
'Fishing a Canadian lake is Mozart,
ocean fishing is Wagner.' Now I think
in a storm, the Saint Lawrence River
is *Götterdämmerung*, some streams
trill Scarlatti, run into head waters,
where I have fished for Gluck,
Debussy, Stravinsky, Shostakovich.
I caught nothing. I still keep fishing
in musical waters: I caught a perch
in a Chinese Lake that was Puccini,
looked exactly like a perch
from the Ashokan Reservoir.
I trapped crustaceans in the River Thames, Purcell –
his flowing theatre and sacred music,
not far from Devil's Acre. A little north,
at Oxfordshire where the Thames (Purcell)
becomes Thomas Tallis, I caught rainbow trout,
Salve Intemerata Sanctus et Benedictus.

*

Missa Solemnis from Bach to Weber
is like fishing for a 'manager fish'
in the Caribbean, where slaves had to save
the best fish for their manager.
Take the Dead Sea, lowest point on earth,
lowering every year – where there's no music
or fish in the sea's murderous salt,
there are bacteria colonies near shore.
Still a diver in full salty gear told me he's heard
someone or something practising
bubbling-bassoon-scales at sea bottom,
'clown of the orchestra', bassoon.
The *Dead Sea Scrolls* may be read
basso profondo, or by castrati
in their lost art. Since we first became human,
when we fished, and hunted, there was music,
love songs much like a leopard's purring,
hands clapped to dance, heel and toe percussions;
mamas hummed wordless music that became lullabies.
Visiting fisherman, I quickstepped barefoot
over sharp Dead Sea stones to swim,
Goddamn, I cut my feet, but
the tough bare-footed Israeli I swam with
stepped and danced on the stones
as if he were in a make-believe ballroom.
I asked him with a smile,
'Do you think your feet might not be Jewish –'
a poet-soldier, he didn't like my joke.

*

I remember how friends swim,
and those who cannot swim,
original and conventional swimmers.
They carried invisible musical instruments.
No beach umbrellas. I netted crawdads
near New Orleans, where the Mississippi
became Bunk Johnson, Louis Nelson Delisle,
Louis Armstrong, Sidney Bechet, the Hot 8,
depending on Ole Miss's mood.

*

Traveller, not Robert E. Lee's horse,
I was an underwater swimmer in Copland's Hudson
without sheet music, mask or snorkel.
I would go down 30 feet, hear the music
of cold water in my ears. Was it Bernstein's *Candide*?
I heard cadenzas, never a full orchestra.
I dived with my dog Sancho after rocks
into a brook, the Bushkill, John Cage –
a dog-man game we both loved.
If Sancho was hunting in the woods,
I didn't have to whistle to call him,
I played opera on a phonograph and he'd come
swimming across the John Cage Bushkill
from the often twelve-toned wilderness
of Schönberg, where Arnold was
the Rondout Reservoir, full of *Sprech Musik*,
between singing and speaking,
a *Pierrot Lunaire* waterfall. Sancho would run
through water music in the Dorian mode,
somewhere between universal Stravinsky's
The Rite of Spring and Debussy's *Sunken Cathedral* –
depending on the season. From a glen,
I saw Satie trickle, refusing to be grand.
I heard Berg and Bartók were flooding in Vienna.
Beauty, I bet my life, is not an entertainment,
it ennobles – contrast, not conflict,
F means *forte*, 'loud', not war. Yes, there is
reiteration, overtones, dissonance, harmony
vs counterpoint. Two melodic lines may go together.

Still there are those who prefer a person's body
on many occasions to his or her art.

The Lamentations of Arthur Krystal

TONY ROBERTS

If you think that Buffy the Vampire Slayer deserves to be the subject of an academic dissertation in English or that the Tarzan books belong in the literary canon because they have been anointed by the Library of America, then you are living at the right time. Elitist literary culture is as defunct as Buffalo Bill, a semi-elitist reference that thirty or forty years ago would have been familiar to serious readers.

AS JEREMIAHS GO, Arthur Krystal is an affable, erudite one, who dispenses his opinions with humour but also with steel. As he explains in *Except When I Write*, he has learned from William Hazlitt: 'In his wonderful essay "The Fight," Hazlitt recalls overhearing one man say to another, "Confound it, man, don't be insipid" and thinking, "that's a good phrase."' Krystal thinks so, too. He does not try to match his master's 'subversive wallop' (nor scorch like Hitchens or garrotte like Epstein) but prefers a tone he once described as provocative but not offensive. Then there is the humour ('I can only speak for the person who brushes my teeth'), the disarming candour ('Like most writers, I seem to be smarter in print than in person') and the literary urbanity ('After all, a Wildean willfulness to be misunderstood underscores one's tastes, adding a certain élan to one's appreciations'). A typical Krystal essay or review balances insight, sense and humour, trawling back through the past of an issue, liberally illustrating it with quotations from interested parties. (For this we forgive him some old targets and the occasional 'judicious repetition' of opinions and references.)

There are now four slim, infinitely quotable books of essays: *Agitations: Essays on Life and Literature* (2002); *The Half-Life of an American Essayist* (2007); *Except When I Write: Reflections of a Recovering Critic* (2011); and slimmest of all, *This Thing We Call Literature* (2016). Krystal (born 1948) is a regular contributor to *The New Yorker* and *Harper's Magazine* among others, where he writes and reviews on any number of subjects, from God to night time. He is also an editor on the work of Jacques Barzun, his teacher, and a screenwriter to boot.

For me, he is at his most interesting as a literary essayist and there he focuses on essentials: 'In short, no art without craft; no craft without individual sensibility; and no art-object without the artist's negotiation between tradition and innovation.' A student of the canonical tradition, his lamentations on the state of literature, like Hazlitt's, begin in personal observation ('the romance of books is swiftly disappearing') and proceed from the premise 'that art has always been the product of talent, skill, inspiration, and labor; and so, to a degree, has been the appreciation of art'. Consequently art is the responsibility both of its creators and its audience. It is Krystal's view that both sides have been failing badly, so badly in fact that the know-nothings, the politically suspect and the mercenary have taken over.

Agitations introduced us to Krystal's perspective on what he has recently called 'this age of diminished expectations', where taste has been reduced to a matter of personal preferences. He caused a stir with the essay 'Closing the Books: A Once-Devoted Reader Arrives at the End of the Story', first published in *Harper's* in 1996 and included here. Essentially Krystal argues there that he can no longer find pleasure, meaning, or merit in literature. He concedes that it is difficult to recapture the excitement of discovery one first has as a young reader and also that our experiences in life dull the impact of like experiences in literature. However, he sees other stifling forces involved. The media has been 'devaluing the idea of privacy' and thereby impoverishing the writer's imagination. Further, the literary climate has been smothered by the academy, 'that confederation of professors and curricula which over the last three decades has reversed the respective status of criticism and belles lettres'.

In 'The Rise and Fall of Theory' we hear that those 'superior' professors saw in 'novels and poems [...] semiotic tracts that reflect all sorts of nasty, royalist, elitist, patriarchal, sexist, and imperialist sympathies'. In cutting the text down to size they served to politicise and further alienate audiences. Yet Krystal reminds us that 'art is not foremost in the business of rectifying injustice or inequality; it is not about the suffering masses. It is about those who are born with a need and a gift to create, and about people whose nature and intelligence compel them to seek and understand such creation'. To Krystal being literary is comparable to being musical, not militant.

Universities are the custodians of literature. In 'What Do You Know?' – on the decline of embarrassment at ignorance – he writes: 'Students are urged to get hip to what "knowledge" and "culture" really signify: the power struggle between classes, races, and sexes.' In 'Death, It's What Ails You', he worries that the remoteness of dead writers seems to be accelerating alarmingly. Not only is Dryden dropped, he argues by way of example, but Milton too, in favour of Stephen King (a popular example with Krystal of someone having greatness thrust upon them). And yet poets also deserve a kicking.

'Going, Going, Gone' turns specifically to the decline of poetry, its modernist practitioners creating a chasm between the 'text' and conventional readers: 'The irony here is that in ridding itself of formal characteristics and adopting free verse to portray the world more realistically, in language approximating the vocabulary and rhythms of ordinary discourse, poetry succeeded in losing what little audience it had left.'

Krystal has been disappointed in print about poetry since at least 1996, feeling that poets are over-hyped, with critics 'assigning greatness where there is only intelligence and competence'. Back then he named names: Helen Vendler, John Ashbery, Rita Dove. Not so in his new book, *This Thing We Call Literature*. 'LISTEN to the Sound It Makes' takes-on the deafness of contemporary poets. He laments the dearth of memorability in modern poetry, which he ascribes to a lack of interest in its musical nature, in the rhythm, the metre. With acknowledged exceptions (Wilbur, Walcott, Heaney at times) he feels the day the music died was somewhere around 1977 and its requiem was Larkin's 'Aubade'.

Paradoxically – and this he acknowledges – Krystal's preference has always been for reading a poem and not for hearing it read aloud. So the music has been internalised: 'the tempo, the emphasis, the feelings are synthesised in us'. The poet's voice is constantly forging the reader's. He does not damn poets for incompetence. In fact he finds 'intelligence, shrewdness, irony, and humour' in many practitioners (some named), but not an interest in music. Krystal's problem with the 'atonal' nature of contemporary poetry is compounded by his sense that continuity has been severed with the past and its poetic wealth. Essentially, as Trilling explained in *Matthew Arnold*, 'Natural magic and moral profundity – these are the two attributes of great poetry.' Krystal can no longer find them.

There is no one way to answer that, unless it is to give lists of the 'musical' poems Krystal omitted to mention. When the essay appeared in *The Chronicle of Higher Education* quite a few of the responders did give lists. One argued hip-hop and rap were the current poetic musical locus; another pointed to the fact that the poets Krystal liked were dead and anthologised and therefore more often seen; another questioned the automatic connection of music with metric regularity. Others might have blamed the universities for turning poetry into metaphysics, or into emails among friends. They might have wondered if perhaps Krystal's own nostalgia has something to do with his beef. At any event, the comments showed there is breath in the argument yet.

It is not Hazlitt, but the spirit of Lionel Trilling – the pre-eminent American literary critic of the middle of the last century – which permeates *This Thing We Call Literature*. Like the 'Closing the Books' essay, it is 'essentially a lament and not a condemnation of the general literary culture' although there *is* condemnation of those who trumpet the new as the great, or elevate the second rate. Creative works are being talked up wildly because of the absence of the real thing, or because it is in the interests of the talkers (critics, professors, publishers, gallery owners) or, as Rebecca Watts argued, on the part of cultural commentators who 'are playing a part in the establishment's muddle-headed conspiracy to "democratise" poetry' (see *PNR* 239 'The Cult of the Noble Amateur'. At numerous times, when reading Krystal, the mind turns to Watts's reasoned argument).

Two essays in the collection deal with genre fiction, those novels 'delivering less rarefied pleasures'. One concerns *Time* magazine's book critic, Lev Grossman's contention that genres are hybridising and hierarchies collapsing, an argument Krystal engages with. (He also interestingly contrasts the opening of Christie's *Murder on the Orient Express* with Ford's *Parade's End* to illustrate how Christie's language wants us to settle in to the narrative, while 'Ford demands that we pay attention'. Krystal also makes the point that anyway enjoyment is not a matter of choosing between the high and low, since quality always comes down to craft: '[Elmore] Leonard

has his skills *and* his place in literature without exactly being part of literature as Trilling understood it.'

Ultimately, though, this high-low business does matter greatly. In 'A Sad Road to Everything', Krystal suggests that the tension which exists between the individual and society is at the heart of what literature is about and that literature 'charts our changing relationship to the issues that intrigue us'. It is vital, therefore, that literary writers 'interrogate reality' to explore the human condition. To break down the barriers to what constitutes serious literature, then, to give everything equivalence as publishers do when sales drive critical reception, is more than worrying. Literature is, to Krystal, what Matthew Arnold called 'a criticism of life'. And if all this smacks of elitism, so what? 'Literature is an art and not meant to be convenient [...] This doesn't automatically exclude the less sophisticated, but it might, and so be it.'

The other elephant in the room is, of course, 'the canon'. The essay 'What is Literature?' begins with a narrative of the canon's history: 'a way of establishing a national literature that would build on the Ancients and vie with other nations'. It was incorporated into university syllabuses in the 1920s, where it held sway until the 1970s and '80s when the so-called 'culture wars' undermined its legitimacy, because of its supposed exclusivity, paternalism, oppressiveness, reverence and hierarchical, patronising nature – in other words its justification of 'the prevailing social order'. Acknowledging that the canon was at least 'exclusionary by nature', 'a result of the middle class's desire to see its own values reflected in art', Krystal comes to its defence 'as a convenient fiction, shaped in part by the material conditions under which writing is produced and consumed, while simultaneously recognising the validity of hierarchical thinking and aesthetic criteria'. We live, inevitably, in a world of Top 20s.

Krystal brings us up to the moment with 'The Shrinking World of Ideas' where he argues, in effect, that science has built a flyover where once stood Trilling's 'dark and bloody crossroads where literature and politics meet'. The Second World War and the Cold War had raised crucial moral issues, which literature, history and philosophy were there to address. Trilling was a proponent, therefore, of the idea that literature was a reason for living. (Now he is seen as 'literature's superego', 'a suffocating ghost' according to Adam Kirsch, in *Why Trilling Matters* (2011).) Even fifty years ago, according to Krystal, 'we opened books not just to learn about the content of a writer's mind but to hear the right words in the right order telling us things we sensed to be true'.

Eventually critical theory derailed the 'humanistic charter' of the arts and now scientific disciplines have triumphed, especially neuroscience because 'our preferences, behaviours, tropes, and thoughts – the very stuff of consciousness – are by-products of the brain's activity'. Where we once saw – with critics like Barzun and Trilling – 'no fissure between moral and aesthetic intelligence', we now see synapses.

Occasionally an Arthur Krystal essay focuses on a single eminent critic. In his new book, his longest essay is a consideration of Erich Auerbach and his seminal work of comparative literature, *Mimesis*, 'the apex of European humanist criticism'. Krystal's presents a well-rounded portrait of a man who seemed to share Dante's sense of tragic destiny, who literally and temperamentally came to be defined by exile and thought, a critic with occasional failings, but a master of the philological approach to literature.

Krystal's interest in Auerbach suggests there is life in high culture yet. If it is defunct, then as Lesley Chamberlain wrote in defence of George Steiner in a recent *TLS*

letter, 'If there are generations out there who have never registered high culture's early twentieth-century objection to democracy's downsides, and the commodification of everything, then they are missing a vital chapter in the history of ideas.'

And yet there is still so much to be argued over in the pages of Arthur Krystal's collections. After all, reading is a serious business –or it should be.

Two Horatian Epistles

JOHN MCAULIFFE

To the Management

after Horace, Epistle 1.14
for David Matthews & Roy Gibson

Manager of my offices and working week,
could we figure out, statistically, which of us does better?
You, grounding strategy in bricks and mortar, or me
tightening the screw on a phrase or an image. Let's try and see
which is the better commanded, my field or yours.

I call that poet lucky who writes at a kitchen table,
following a line, leaning into its every tautening. *You* call
blessed the one who has gotten away. But your *dullsville*
I walk around like a lord: on tree-lined dusty side-roads
the goldfinches' arrival, or a tide of copper leaves,
can tempt me into detours. And when I arrive,
never late, at my local, there's a friendly face,
Ceefax in one corner on a small screen and no 'next
big thing' in the offing. (Envying another
is to hate your own place, and know no other.)

When you lived in the capital, slavishly filling in forms,
analysing data for reports, you dreamed
of going home to the provinces with new knowledge.
Now, you long for bright lights, a famous face
made out on the underground. Stuck here, you cut
and paste the formal requirements, doing
what you're told. This is your life, to wear
a suit that won't be outshone by the accountants,
(and yes I like the cut of those unstructured, wide-leg outfits),
to discover figures that will survive an audit, to pluck outcomes
from colleagues who hadn't planned for them, who resist
every innovation, and whose wisdom is to wait
on five-year cycles and a change of minister. Money,

money, money. What you are proud of, I can see:
the shining hair, toned body and snazzy specs (which start
to look a little dated now, like everything futuristic)
that got you in the door at the capital's clubs.
Famous night schools and a society you'd only ever heard of
are fondly 'recalled', over flat whites
at whichever chain just rented the corner site
at our campus's dead margin. But,
such foolishness is ok over a simple meal. I know.

When I robe up and read out the students' names
at the end-of-year ceremony, doffing my silly hat and
mispronouncing every other unusually accented name,
my neighbours laugh. There, but for the grace of god. I join in,
while you are anxious, looking at your watch, measuring out
small talk, cursing fate, the latest message putting you on edge,
dreaming more and more of the Royal Mile.

It is half accident and some design, the easy life I live,
and will always return happily to, tanned, as you will see,
and with a taste for the fine balance of Occitan reds. I have,
once in a while, thought I'd fit in at the oval tables you sit at,
poring over figures, filtering, recombining...
but this dumb ox, making lines in his narrow field,
would not be happy to have, best outcome, his head turned
by some stranger from the court decreeing
'What a fox!'
                        Awkward as the fit might be,
and knowing where these lines are going –
I can say 'nowhere' as quick as anyone! –
I stand over their numbering days, searching for occasion
in every leaf that falls to earth.

Naming the Days

after Horace, 3.8

The 31st, and I'm free, almost idle,
paid in full and logged off, sending smoke
across the real, burning for connections –
Call over,

I was thinking, my learnéd friend,
and here you are: let's offer
something up, to living well and days
on which the axe won't fall.

Spring's begun again with sunlight on hail,
brightness surfacing
and extending into night.
This Sangiovese

has had time to breathe so, if you love me,
raise your glass,
to the lights we live by
and their long finish. The vote

is a disaster, you're right,
and likewise this city, the country,
even love and books,
the starry realms shining above us

with glorious has-beens, secret sharers,
informants, dealers, priests
and their satellites
who are planning, soon, but not yet

another life. Write, *So be it*
as the world turns. To yourself, as they say,
and nights that, in the foolish light of day,
won't foster regret.

after Ithaka: Five Beds, Respiratory Ward

LISA KELLY

1.

Mary is waiting, breathing and waiting,
breathing shallowly, waiting and waiting
for a breeze to carry her vessel to the Brompton.
A sea-sick shanty, *I'm going to the Brompton,*
soon I'll be setting out for the Brompton,
all my notes are at the Brompton.
Nurse, is there any news from the Brompton?
But Mary is moored to her oxygen tubing,
today there is no fair passage to the Brompton,
so while she is waiting, I take her comb
and scratch her back under her gown
where there is an itch she cannot reach
and she is itching, itching, itching,
itching to get underway for the Brompton.

2.

With each breath, Jenny's lung tumours move.
Now one cowers on her spine. When she moves,
like a Cyclops's eye, it looks to make her shrink.
Soon radiotherapy will make it shrink.
What you bring inside your soul can make you shrink.
I'm on a journey. I've never for one moment shrunk,
never thought 'why me'. I'm not going to shrink.
I'm 53, my first grandchild is due. I'll prove
I can beat this. Her thoughts raised high to not shrink
her rare excitement. I ask about her long road.
She has plans for her business, a partner to share the load.
It will be full of discovery – alternative therapies,
adventures with the family. *I will try everything to remove*
these tumours. This is my journey. I will not shrink.

3.

Kate slipped when the paddling pool spilled over
and angry Poseidon threw her over
onto her back. Cracked two ribs. She doesn't know
how long she was out for. Her granddaughter didn't know
why granny slept on the wet patio, didn't know
who to call. The two-year old brother knew
nothing, curled up like a shell inside, can't now know
granny's lungs are filled with fluid, how she never
thought she'd spend her birthday here. *Who'd ever know?*
I look at her cake, packets of biscuits, sweating fruit.
They mean well, but I'll not be eating any of that.
Swabbed for a bacterium like flesh-eating Laestrygonians,
she is queasy about what she might encounter.
When can I go home is what I'd really like to know.

4.

She is dreaming, sleeping and dreaming,
hardly stirring, dreaming and dreaming
of summer mornings when she can watch
a harbour come into view, sit on the quay, watch
traders lift fine things to tempt her – rugs, watches,
and as she dreams her parents are on watch,
the rise and fall of her breath ticks like an erratic watch.
Her mother applies perfumed creams, massaging
the length of her arms in long strokes, watches
for a flicker of pleasure. I look away,
learn from a nurse, *She's in for a long stay.*
It's her heart. When her family departs,
she goes on with her journey. Hope it's enriching,
hope she is so full of experience. We can only watch.

5.

This is my stop-over, this is my new crew
in the same clichéd boat. Hello new crew.
Hello all the doctors and nurses in our lives,
in and out, in and out of our lives as if we live
at one of the world's busiest ports. We live
and breathe not particularly well, but we live,
so that's a start. Are we destined to live?
What is true for all voyagers who
seek a long road are times when we live
like voyeurs. We watch each other in open seas,
wonder about all these Ithakas, ease
our understandings into different landings.
I take my mother-of-pearl pills, lips no longer blue,
sailing on, not fooled, richer for sharing lives.

Two Poems

LIZ LEFROY

A Minor Loss of Fidelity

We bruise into the party in our plumage – I said, *Dress up!* and you overdid it,
always one to take the pink to its literal limit. You're beautiful:
the gathering can hardly stand me either and it shows, the way guests stand aside,
grope for more bitter with their other hands. We uncork our prosecco.

You said, as we stopped on the way to buy our emergency sandwiches:
Always take what you want to drink to a party, or what you don't,
and either way, hold on tight to your glass. The man on the checkout agreed,
said he'd have thrown in his number if it wasn't against the rules.

You've taught me nearly everything I know, so when that woman
– the one who's almost good-looking – hits on you, I ignore her husband
standing three feet away, ignore her unmissable red-soaked lips.

I think she thought she could get away with it, this slipping out early,
brushing her hand on a woman's arse, as if no one understands such a thing
in this district; as if to say, *Darling, I'm only saying it like it could be!*

Your Shadow at Evening Rising to Meet You

When the invigilator calls time,
she picks up her pen,
undoes all she's said of Eliot.

It takes three hours to clean the page.

At the words, *You may begin*,
she leaves the hall, slips
silently through the knot
of anxious girls,
walks down the slope
towards the Finchley Road,
to the sound of horns and motors,
taxis waiting.

At the station, the barrier opens,
feeds out her ticket.
The carriage closes weary doors
behind her, reverses through
Baker Street towards King's Cross.

Reaching the other end she breaks the rules,
wrong-foots the escalator,
walks through the thickening trees.

He is standing on the doorstep,
wearing a knee-length dressing gown.
He tries again to kiss her
as they manoeuvre back into the house.
She follows him to the bedroom
where he sits, naked now,
on the narrow bed.

He watches as she takes off her shoes,
lifts her crumpled blouse.

Exploring the Supernatural Lapse of Time in Fairyland and General Relativity Theory

How modern poetry plays with space and time, and lives on the edges

EMILY GROSHOLZ

I FEEL LUCKY that I live close to where I grew up, on the outskirts of Philadelphia. I still have quite a few cousins there, and friends from high school, and my youngest son just graduated from Haverford College, so I drive by my old house rather often. It is right next to a big Catholic Church, Our Lady of the Assumption, flanked by a rectory for the priests, a primary school and a garden-like cemetery which always seemed to me like a bit of Italy. The church bought our house (a decade or so after my father left it), and turned it into offices; the resident priest was very nice, so I could take my children in there, and show them my favourite places. One such place was the modest landing-stair where the front staircase turned a corner in the way down. I liked to plant myself there and observe. Perhaps I was inspired by the poem 'Halfway Down', by A. A. Milne, which I learned from a brightly coloured vinyl record; it was turned into a song which I can and do frequently sing out loud. If you go on YouTube, you can here that very song performed by Robin the Frog (Kermit's nephew!) and also by Gene Kelly, looking debonair:

Halfway down the stairs
Is a stair
Where I sit.
There isn't any
Other stair
Quite like
It.

I'm not at the bottom,
I'm not at the top;
So this is the stair
Where
I always
Stop.

Halfway up the stairs
Isn't up
And isn't down.
It isn't in the nursery,
It isn't in the town.
And all sorts of funny thoughts
Run round my head.
'It isn't really
Anywhere!
It's somewhere else
Instead!'

The poem is from his collection *When We Were Very Young* (Milne, 1924–61). I remember that stair as a middle term between the upstairs and the downstairs, between my room and the world outside, a place where no adult would ever sit. I spent a lot of time there, imagining. It had a family resemblance to the windowsill of my room, where I waited expectantly for Peter Pan to appear on the threshold between my house and Neverland, and to the back of my closet, where I supposed that one day the back wall would become a door to Narnia. I waited and waited, losing track of time; the otherworld was there and not there, always close at hand but requiring magic for access. But who has reliable mastery of magic, except the odd wizard, like Gandalf or (later) Dumbledore?

So when I first read Keats's 'La Belle Dame sans Merci' and Yeats's 'Song of the Wandering Aengus', and, years later, Yves Bonnefoy's memoir *L'Arrière pays* (Bonnefoy 2003), I recognised the protagonists immediately, young mortals entranced by the transient light of a shade, the beam that lights up and makes sombre whatever it rests upon: 'a glimmering girl / With apple blossoms in her hair, / Who called me by my name and ran, / And vanished in the darkening air,' with whom one hopes to 'pluck till time and times are done / The silver apples of the moon, / The golden apples of the sun.' Back to YouTube: listen to Donovan's lovely rendition of this poem as a song.

Using Stith Thompson's celebrated *Motif-Index of Folk-Literature*, we might classify all of these poems with Walter Map's King Herla and Washington Irvings's *Rip Van Winkle* under F377, 'Supernatural Lapse of Time in Fairyland'. The combined proximity and inaccessibility of the other world does something odd to temporality; often those who briefly stray into fairyland and then return home find that centuries have passed (Thompson, 1955–58). This might remind you of the 'Twin Paradox' that stems from Special Relativity Theory: when one of two identical twins goes off in a spaceship at close to the speed of light, he returns home a few years later to discover that his brother is an old man. C. S. Lewis offers an inverse magic in his books: again and again, months or even years spent in Narnia, and great voyages across its seas and mountains, return the Pevensie children to the same house and day on which they departed.

The seeds of Einstein's cosmological revolution may be located in James Clerk Maxwell's set of partial differential equations that laid the foundation of classical electrodynamics and optics. Einstein postulated the invariance of the velocity of light c in a vacuum as a result of studying Maxwell's results, and then thought through the consequences of this insight in relation to Galilean relativity (the claim that inertial motion, straight line motion at a constant speed, is physically equivalent to rest). In his 'Theory of Special Relativity' (1905), the first of his revolutionary theories, he argued that Newton's notions of absolute time as well as of absolute simultaneity were untenable. While time in the theory of special relativity was no longer absolute, however, the space-time framework was still rigid, a fixed 'stage' within which physical events simply take place. Based on the failure of scientists to detect any changes in the relative velocity of light, Einstein posited that the speed of light in a vacuum c will be the same for all inertial frames, and thus the relative speed between moving bodies could never be accelerated beyond the speed of light. He realised that if we pursue consistently the implications of Galilean invariance in a Leibnizian way (all uniform motion is relative and there are no privileged inertial reference frames) together with the invariance of the speed of light, consequences unforeseen by Newtonian mechanics – and of course barred by Newton's insistence on absolute space and time – must follow. The duration of the time interval between two events, and what counts as a set of simultaneous events, for example, will not be the same for all observers, so that talk of space and time must become talk of four dimensional spacetime; and energy and mass will be equivalent, that is, $E = mc^2$.

Einstein's second revolution, the theory of general relativity (1915), resulted from Einstein's attempt to unify special relativity with a theory of gravity. Einstein was motivated in this work by two seemingly simple observations. Abhay Ashtekar notes:

First, as Galileo demonstrated through his famous experiments at the leaning tower of Pisa, the effect of gravity is universal: all bodies fall the same way if the only force on them is gravitational. Second, gravity is always attractive. This is in striking contrast with, say, the electric force where unlike charges attract while like charges repel. As a result, while one can easily create regions in which the electric field vanishes, one cannot build gravity shields. Thus, gravity is omnipresent and non-discriminating; it is everywhere and acts on everything the same way. These two facts make gravity unlike any other fundamental force, and suggest that gravity is a manifestation of something deeper and universal. (2015)

Since space-time is also omnipresent, Einstein came to see gravity and space-time as expressions of the same cosmic structure: space-time is curved by the presence of matter and it is dynamic; the effects of gravity explain, and are explained by, the curvature of space-time. So time in general relativity becomes 'elastic': whereas in special relativity time intervals depend on the motion of the observer, in general relativity they can also depend on the location of the observer, because of variable curvature.

One philosophical consequence of Einstein's theories and their postulation of space-time is the hypothesis of the 'block universe', which claims that all existence in time is equally real; it is not just the present moment that is real, and the reality of the future is no different from the reality of the past. This hypothesis chimes both with the human experience of vivid memories, and with the aims of art: art aims to be unforgettable. This is why poets make their poems beautiful and impose various kinds of periodicity upon them, which also explains why poems are so often turned into song. Here is one of my favourite poems by A. E. Housman.

Into my heart an air that kills
    From yon far country blows:
What are those blue remembered hills,
    What spires, what farms are those?

That is the land of lost content,
    I see it shining plain,
The happy highways where I went
    And cannot come again.

Those blue remembered hills. In many European paintings, the colour blue is the sign of distance, and the edges of a landscape are tinted blue; but that habit also brings them to our attention and makes them beautiful. When we remember the past, the vivid past that we may long for, inhabited by people we may long for, it is still there, real and compelling. It could be a place nearby (like my house on the outskirts of Philadelphia, still there but lacking most of its beautiful ambient trees and my old family) or a place far away (like my vanished courtyard in Paris, replaced by an ugly high-rise in Belleville): but there it is. I see it shining plain.

It is there but not there, like Messier 51, the Whirlpool Galaxy, whose picture taken by the Hubble Telescope up in space I just inserted in my new book *Great Circles* in the chapter where I discuss cosmological poems. The Whirlpool Galaxy is twenty-three million light years from Earth, so that lovely picture is in fact the record of the galaxy as it was twenty-three million years ago. I suppose it is still there; it would take us another twenty-three million years to go visit it and see how it is doing. Some consequences of Einstein's General Relativity Theory, in combination with Henrietta Swan Leavitt's identification and documentation of Cepheid Variables (Standard Candles), and Hubble's collection of astronomical data informed by Einstein's theory and Leavitt's empirical insight, is that our universe is much bigger than we thought and it is dynamic (seems to be expanding from the Big Bang). Indeed, there are, not one or two, but one or two billion galaxies. Of course, it is just the light emitted from Messier 51 that we see in the Hubble photograph, which can only travel at the speed of light, as it is only photographs from 1950 or 1980 that record in the same way my old house and its trees, or my courtyard in Paris.

So the 'block universe' philosophical theory isn't confirmed by the Hubble photograph, though it does have some support in modern cosmological theory. However, in terms of our human experience, it is problematic. We think we are free, so that what we might have done but did not do has a kind of ontological status: that is the basis of our ethical life. And we long for the past because of family bonds, friendship and eros. In Keats's 'La Belle Dame sans Merci' and Yeats's 'Song of the Wandering Aengus', fairyland is marked by eros. In Yeats's 'The Wild Swans at Coole', and in the great elegies at the end of *The Tempest* (Act 4, scene 1, and Epilogue) there is renunciation, which depends on choice, expressed in 'performative utterance': Yeats abjures Maude Gonne, and Shakespeare-Prospero abjures his art. But being free, the ability to act, the acknowledgment of unrealised possibles, depend on a future that cannot be foreseen, and that is modally different from the past. It also depends on a sense of the absolute value of existence, of the beloved, of oneself and other human beings, of the earth and its creatures. Another version of fairyland is the great dome of heaven, and the earthy paradise posed on a mountaintop, blessing the lives that continue beneath them. Another is the forest, the wild on the edge of civilisation, as in Shakespeare's *A Midsummer Night's Dream*. Another is the underworld down the rabbit-hole, where Lewis Carroll's Alice slides, or the tiny planet, poised on a clover, where Dr Seuss's Whos live in Whoville. The 'block universe' of space-time tells us the asymmetry of time is an illusion, so that nothing is lost in time and space, so there is no point in visiting the edges, in watching for the passage to fairyland, the adjacent reality that changes the meaning of the here and now. However, that claim seems incompatible with some of the most important aspects of human life, which often are precisely those that inspire poetry.

The poetic tales that fall under Stith Thompson's Folk Motif F377 not only bend time, they also cast a shadow on the real world, the world we think we live in. The shadow is not mere illusion; those moments halfway between, those ambiguous places that confound the usual categories, places where no grownup would ever sit (except perhaps some poets, or some mathematicians), reveal something crucial. Why does Keats's pale knight-at-arms go on loitering there by the lake, where the sedge has withered and no birds sing? He has been disillusioned by the lovely and musical fairy, but he cannot give her up. And Yeats in 'Among School Children' revives Maude Gonne again, as a child and as the old woman she has become, and then turns her, or perhaps his song for her, into a tree with a kind of mortal immortality:

> Labour is blossoming or dancing where
> The body is not bruised to pleasure soul,
> Nor beauty born out of its own despair,
> Nor blear-eyed wisdom out of midnight oil.
> O chestnut tree, great rooted blossomer,
> Are you the leaf, the blossom or the bole?
> O body swayed to music, O brightening glance,
> How can we know the dancer from the dance?

Yves Bonnefoy suggests something similar, in his poem 'To the Voice of Kathleen Ferrier', the great English contralto who died tragically in 1953 at the age of forty-one, which I offer in my own translation:

> All gentleness and irony converged
> For this farewell of crystal and low clouds,
> Thrustings of a sword played upon silence,
> Light that glanced obscurely on the blade.
>
> I celebrate the voice blended with grey
> That falters in the distances of singing
> As if beyond pure form another song's
> Vibrato rose, the only absolute.
>
> O light and light's denial, smiling tears
> That shine upon both anguish and desire,
> True swan, upon the water's dark illusion,
> Source, when evening deepens and descends.
>
> You seem to be at home on either shore,
> Extremes of happiness, extremes of pain.
> And there among the luminous grey reeds
> You seem to draw upon eternity.

Here I translate Bonnefoy; he translated many poems by

Yeats, which is another kind of revival, another homage to the mortal immortality of poetry and song; and he wrote an especially wonderful essay about 'Among School Children', which I have translated.

Poems not only have an odd effect on time, bending not only time but space as well, evoking and poetically exploiting our human habits of vision, which I suppose vindicates Einstein, as well as William Blake:

> To see a World in a Grain of Sand
> And a Heaven in a Wild Flower,
> Hold Infinity in the palm of your hand
> And Eternity in an hour.

So let us turn to different aspects of human experience that lurk at the edges of ordinary life, there and not there, changing the meaning of what happens. There is the very large, starred above, the great dome of heaven, and the circle of the sea, which is also the circle of the horizon, where we are travelling by foot or boat. There is the very small, below or within, the cauldron from which living things boil up. There is the past, which often brings the far-away close, along with what might have happened, but did not.

Julia Randall urges us to sit still and contemplate, clearing the mind of distractions so that it can see truly, that is, penetrate to essences in a moment free of succession. She tries to recover form out of a perennial centre, writing that art is a light 'which illuminates wider and wider areas of our obscure existence: the next and next room of the single dream'. The genre of poetry that attracted her was the meditative or mystical lyric; she had no penchant for either narrative or argument that depends on temporal and logical succession, no need for getting somewhere. She was where she was, under the shadow of Hershfield's Hill, past Dougherty's fields, by Long Green Branch in a corner of Maryland between Chesapeake and the Shenandoah range.

What does she mean by the moment of illumination? Spiritual danger follows upon a mismatch of the inside and outside of things, the invisible and visible, the subjective and objective. A poet who is attentive and undistracted can speak truly by achieving an adamic state, in the earthly paradise where the innocent mind confronts things as they are essentially, where natural or technical form and psychic form coincide. The work of art expresses this union in the moment of illumination and so is the locus, the topos, of truth. Here, wisdom is intuitive, not discursive; solitary and visionary, not social; still, not peripatetic. So too, she generally tries to minimise the successiveness of her poems so that they will appear as if present all at once, by creating a phonic texture that is particularly rich in consonance, assonance and rhyme. Precisely because these phonic units have no semantic import, they cannot be developed; rather, they are just the same element upon each reappearance and so pull all the parts of the poem where they occur back into the same timeless moment. Succession is subordinated to and masked by sheer repetition.

Randall's vision does not obscure the particularity of place, but imposes upon it that mark of the transcendent, absolute significance. Her corner of Maryland is, for Randall, the place most rich in resonances, already covered like a coral reef with the accretions of a lifetime. The soul, brought home by the discipline of contemplation, knows where it is in virtue of where it is not, so that Elsewhere may become, by the process of poetic compression, aspects of the local scene:

> Somewhere, Sir Thomas Browne,
> In a friend's face, dying, saw a ghost of bone
> Rise, and the family feature
> Clear off the curves of earned, familiar nature:
> Lusts, comforts, every lineament of school,
> Or private light of industry or travel.
> Pure Peter vanished, and the patient lay
> Pure Willoughby, pure Cameron, family clay
> Startled to reclamation. Then if place,
> Too, is our ancestor (that is
> The forever England concept), this low east,
> Like love, rides in the gesture of my flesh.
>
> Green Appalachian must outlast
> Apennine or Sierra – even the sun
> That struck on Shasta while we ate
> Lunch, and the hoary marmots watched, or even
> Dust on that mountain steeper than the way
> From Lerici to Turbia. Cardinal
> Cannot turn to nightingale, wisteria come
> Hawthorne or oleander, nor I root
> Far from Patapsco's ledges, or Wye's foot.
>   ('Maryland')

Randall is always interested in the singular occasion which, though it can be revisited in memory, happens only once. In 'Rockland', an old house becomes a poetic subject just as its time is up, on the sole, sad day of its vacating. In 'A Farewell to History', a marriage is summed up and dismissed in the bloody fight that ended it. The domestic round is described from the vantage of its interruptions or its demise: in 'A Ballad of Eve', Eve contends that what makes us human was her disruptive act, once and for all, that broke the quotidian pattern of Eden:

> And there upon the bough it lay,
> That made my first heart break.
> With human hands I plucked the sky,
> With human hunger ate.

The paradigm of an unrepeatable act is the creation of the work of art; the work itself becomes permanent testimony to the incursion of something absolute into mere succession:

> Bearded to match his willow, he sits here
> By his pond. It is always summer. Far away
> Ice cracks the jetties, holy towers fall,
> The Channel rages. Let the world be done.
>
> In the quiet of the lilies, never won
> Since Eden rose and the archangel fell,
> That battle with the light goes on and on.
>   ('Giverny')

What is brought here to steadfast expression is Monet's moment of illumination where subject and object (his beard, the willows; his willows, the painted willows; his inner peace and the quiet lilies; his battle with the light and the painted lilies) finally correspond.

But without succession, Randall's poetry is sometimes trapped by a Parmenidean fixity, too self-same and unbecoming to serve as a model of human wholeness:

> Take stones for blood
> Take stance for prophecy
> Take earth for Adam, as it was
> In the beginning
>
> Before the slant Isaiahs in the porch,
> Before the Sibyls, or Theresa like a torch
> Singer, before hair
> Bewildered Magdala;
>
> Or after, perhaps, such holocaust –
> Wordwounded flesh
> Contortioned in a glass – there comes to
> Mind a silence, such as those who sought
> Stunning Medusa found.
>
> Purged of the quest, they stand
> Sentinel, before breath
> Cripples God's hand.
>   ('For Henry Moore')

She says it herself: the mirror of art must be a living mirror, not one that kills and fixes by over-idealisation, by the lure of too-great perfection. Thus, in one of her liveliest, most charming and most serious poems, 'To William Wordsworth in Virginia', Randall acknowledges and abjures the danger. Mere words, the magical resolutions of art, are not sufficient:

> Words that split the tide
> Apart for Moses (not for Mahon's bus),
> Words that say, the bushes burn for us –
> Lilac, forsythia, orange, Sharon rose.
> For us the seasons wheels, the lovers wait,
> All things become the flesh of our delight,
> The evidence of our wishes.

Such wishful vision must be tempered by the acknowledgment of mortality, and the contradictions, the moral depths, of the world as it is. Randall addresses herself to Wordsworth, the musical idealist, the narrator of his own life:

> But, sir, I am tired of living in a lake
> Among the watery weeds and weedy blue
> Shadows of flowers that Hancock never grew.
> I am tired of my wet wishes, of running away
> Like all the nymphs, from the droughty eye of day.
> Run, Daphne, run, Europa, Io, run!
> There is not a god left underneath the sun
> To balk, to ride, to suffer, to obey.
> Here is the unseasonable barberry.
> Here is the black face of a child in need.
> Here is the bloody figure of a man.
> Run, Great Excursioner. Run if you can.

The poet who so often looks down, to the soil and the compost heap, to the vital cells that hatch us, is Maxine Kumin. So, let's first look at the way she writes about beans and peas. She notes: 'Peas prefer to stand alone, unweeded between and crowding in on each other for support before they start to climb the wire fencing. Respectfully, I paper only between their rows to keep out interlopers.' And, 'Green beans, for example, like warm soil, but want to be mulched before summer's full heat strikes.' This part of her essay 'Jicama Without Expectations', is funny, because the paper she uses to shore up her garden are pages from the *New York Times*. She reminds us that it is not easy to be a middle term, up on the hillside above the house and very close to the forest. 'A vegetable garden [...] clearly needs to be fenced and re-fenced. To keep down weeds that take tenacious hold in, around, and through the original buried chicken wire fence and the later additions of hardware cloth, screening and other exotica thrown into the breach when emergencies arise, fat sections of the *Times* can be stuffed into the gaps and pleats, then mulched for appearance's sake.' All the news that's fit to print, informing and protecting the garden.

But when Kumin writes poems about peas and beans, they often turn into people! Or rather, they evoke people, but with that peculiar poetic transmutation that I've always liked in her poetry, her poetic figures migrate into the people they evoke. Here is an example, where she evokes Thoreau, and then her husband Victor.

BEANS
    ... making the earth say beans instead of grass –
this was my daily work. — Thoreau, *Walden*

Having planted
that seven-mile plot
he came to love it
more than he had wanted.
His own sweat
sweetened it.
Standing pat
on his shadow
hoeing every noon
it came to pass
in a summer long gone
that Thoreau
made the earth say beans
instead of grass.

You, my gardener
setting foot
among the weeds
that stubbornly reroot
have raised me up
into hellos
expansive as
those everbearing rows.

Even without
the keepsake strings
to hold the shoots
of growing things
I know this much:

I say beans
at your touch.

Suddenly, the cleverly half-rhymed, two stress, short-short lines produce, from the seeds of a meditation on Thoreau, a love poem! And we find the same erotic play opening 'In the Pea Patch': 'These as they clack in the wind / saying castanets, saying dance with me, / saying do me, dangle their intricate / nuggety scrota [...]'.

In an essay entitled 'Jam enough for a Lifetime', Kumin remembers that when her mother came to visit, she would help with stripping and boiling the berries, because she was used to the tasks of transforming fruit into food and those tasks happily recalled her childhood: 'There was the cold cellar, there stood the jars of pickled beets, the Damson plum conserve larded with hazelnuts: there, too, the waist-high barrel of dill pickles weighted down with three flatirons atop a washtub lid.' But her mother was no longer there, as we only learn at the end of the essay:

My mother would go home from her summer visits with a package of pickles and jams for her later delectation. When she died, there were several unopened jars in her cupboard. I took them back with me after the funeral. We ate them in her stead, as she would have wanted us to. Enough jam for a lifetime, she would say with evident satisfaction after a day of scullery duty. It was; it is.

So she is there, in the essay; and so is Kumin, who died in 2014. And there she is again, busy at the same task, accompanied and alone, in a poem dedicated to her daughter Judith. 'Making the Jam without You', is one of Kumin's empty nest poems, which I have come to appreciate all the more in the last few years. It begins:

Old daughter, small traveler
asleep in a German featherbed
under the eaves in a postcard town
of turrets and towers,
I am putting a dream in your head.

Listen! Here it is afternoon.
the rain comes down like bullets.
I stand in the kitchen,
that harem of good smells
where we have bumped hips and
cracked the cupboards with our talk
while the stove top danced with pots
and it was not clear who did
the mothering. Now I am
crushing the blackberries
to make the annual jam
in a white cocoon of steam

So her daughter too is there and is not there, studying abroad in three languages, but luckily in a place where there are also berries, and young men to cook up 'that tar-thick boil / love cannot stir down'. So then the mother discreetly withdraws, and the poem ends, so the daughter can continue on her own.

And then she is fixing up the beans in the garden with Yann, Judith's son: he is really there:

My grandson and I are doing up the beans
Together to be blanched, then frozen.
We are singing beans beans beans
They make you feel so mean
On the farm on the farm.
Last week he shaved his head at soccer camp
– immediate regret – already it
Is fuzzing over with biracial curls.
The green beans are Provider, bush. The yellow,
Kentucky Wonder, pole. The way I sort
Is for convenience: size, not species.
They make a lovely mix, as do Yann's genes.
I like to think someday the world will be
One color, more or less. The word
Is heterosis, hybrid vigor,
From the Greek for alteration

When Kumin put up her fruits and vegetables, they ended up in her cellar, where they rested side by side with winter vegetables that weren't processed, just keeping cool. 'In the Root Cellar' is as funny in its own way as the essay where the garden is wreathed in the *New York Times*: all the vegetables become characters, some more recognisable than others. You can actually hear her reading it at https://voca.arizona.edu/readings-list/17/20. When she reads it, it is even funnier:

The parsnips, those rabbis
have braided their beards together
to examine the text. The word
that engrosses them is: February.

To be a green tomato
wrapped in the Sunday book section
is to know nothing. Meanwhile
the wet worm eats his way outward.

These cabbages, these clean keepers
in truth are
a row of impacted stillbirths.
One by one we deliver them.

O potato, a wink of
daylight and you're up with
ten tentative erections.
How they deplete you!

Dusty blue wart hogs, the squash
squat for a thump and a tuning.
If we could iron them out
they'd be patient blue mandolins.

The beets wait wearing their birthmarks.
They will be wheeled into the amphitheater.
Even before the scrub-up, the scapel,
they bleed a little.

I am perfect, breathes the onion.
I am God's first circle
the tulip that slept in his navel.
Bite me and be born.

There is the circle again, but this time it is an onion, in the earth! This poem shows that Kumin had a flare for imagism and surrealism, which, subdued by her allegiance to the real world and its creatures, she rarely indulged. But that flare often burns around the edges of her poem, and gives them an unearthly glow even as they blossom, like a New Hampshire sunset behind a grove of apple trees. This reminds me of the woods behind my house, though they are composed not of apple trees, but of maple, oak, black walnut, dogwood, redbud, and birch. Sometimes they become the Clerestory of Chartres, where you can see heaven in the stained glass, as I often did through the playroom windows, while I was nursing the babies:

Awake before dawn, William and I sit drowsing,
Lapsed from a dream, louring toward consciousness,
Nursing a little, musing, counting our toes.
There are always ten, no matter where we begin.
Oh, look. He suddenly points at the closed door-windows
That cast over snow, past spindly lank silhouettes
Of maple, oak, black walnut, into the dawn.

On tiptoe, weaving, he runs up close to the windows
Charmed by the panels of gold set high among mullions
Of boles, the roses fastened in tracery-branches.
Yet how the fastening ravels: our matins are sung,
The windows beyond the windows wither away,
And then he returns to my arms asking his questions
In an ancient, unknown tongue. And all of my answers,
Equally enigmatic, are kisses in shadow.

There is my youngest son, almost 23 years ago! And there is my daughter, who shows up as a snowdrop:

Snow fell so early this year, just after Allhallows,
We never finished the ritual of raking clean
Livid grass and cushions of stricken moss.
The yard's still matted with leaves, oak, maple, walnut,
Visible once again as the snow recedes,
Tatted lace unravelling, going wherever the snows
Of yesteryear retire to, heaven or hellward.
Under the mat of crisscrossed mahogany
And black gold crusted with ice, one snowdrop thaws.

She stands already in the outmost bed, bordering
Woods, though it is only February, turned,
Dear Mary-Frances, less than a week ago. I laid
The coverlet of leaves aside and there she was,
Furled on herself and bowed, but blooming hard,
Sober, exquisite child of an uncertain season.

That poem not only turned into a song, but also a dance, in Japan! But where, where are the children? She has moved to Boston to start her first job, and he has gone to the Atlantic coast of France, to teach English there for a year. Where did they go?

Sometimes my old boyfriend from high school (and his wife and daughter) showed up back there, because his uncle and aunt happened to live right behind our house. He turned the oaks and maples into 'half-golden aspen trees', because of the letters he wrote me sometime during the 1970s, when he lived on a Bodhi in New Mexico:

Six acres on Jemez Cree, which runs between

The constellated hot springs of the canyon
At night in the autumn air, now growing colder,
I sit beneath that other milky way
Alone, in water hotter than my blood.
The place belonged before to Benedictines,
Buildings mostly low, built of adobe;
Large community kitchen, dining hall,
Rooms for meditation, pottery workshed,
Greenhouse, orchards, and outlying fields.
All day we hear the fluid sound of wind
Through the by now half-golden aspen trees,
And lighter music of running water, winding
Only a dozen yards from where I sleep.

And now my oldest son Ben lives in Taos! And his next-younger brother Robbie? He's still around, but mostly studying for medical school and hanging out with his girlfriend who is, like Kumin, an accomplished horsewoman.

Indeed, sometimes Maxine Kumin shows up there in the backyard, because I always sent her messages about the wildflowers as they came up in the spring:

ELEGY
On February first, I went outside
Stepping through pot-cheese snow to look for sprouts,
And there they were,
The tiny dark green tips of snowdrop-spears.

I took a snapshot with my pocket camera,
Intending to print it up
And send it north as I do every year
To let you know that spring is coming soon,
A little earlier here than it arrives
At your New England farm
Perched high against the hillside, house and barn,
Vegetable patch and meadows and dark pond.

Now it is April. February, March
Were lost to ice-storms, blizzards, inland squalls,
And those small stunted sprouts
Could only freeze and unfreeze, freeze again
And wait till April broke: now here they are.
But you were lost before I had a chance
To send your picture north.

Now I could send you flowers,
Dozens of snowdrops starting up in wreathes,
And next to them the striped and dimly starred
And gilded crocuses,
And fast behind the budding daffodils –
Phallic, I think you'd say,
Pleased by the blunt irreverence of saying:
Upwards! Inverse to scrota dangling down,
Those metaphoric green beans in your garden.

They're blooming anyway and everywhere!
And where are you? Who should be here to meet them,
To cast your practiced eye
On my unkempt, unprincipled backyard,
And on this poem that I might have sent
Except I wrote it down because you're gone.

And so too does Yves Bonnefoy. Their visits are always a surprise! I was in the middle of translating Bonnefoy's essay on Yeats when he died:

AT THE EDGE OF THE WOODS
I open the window-door:
There you are at the edge
Where my border of daffodils
Mix with their wild cousins,
Trillium, yellow borage,
Who creep in from the woods
Cross-hatched behind the house.

They come back at the end
Of winter, like the feral cats
We feed and sometimes shelter,
The cardinals and jays
Who fly their colors skyward,
And the striped chipmunks,
'Our plain neighbors,' as you wrote.

They spend the winter underground,
Dreaming of the light, until
They rise. And there you are, again,
Just where the garden blends
Into the mild wilderness of trees.
I call your name; you turn,
Lifting your hand, and smile.

When I was translating *Beginning and End of the Snow*, I was charmed by the way Bonnefoy appreciated the snow in the woods near Williams College, and the great woods stretching up through Canada, and the way he called the chipmunks 'our plain neighbours', as if they were small Amish squirrels.

Come to think of it, Fred Morgan is in there too, in the midst of a great snow shower, in 'The House of Trees':

In summer it's a mansion of green rooms
Whose walls of woven honeysuckle border,
Flank of walnut, buttress of wild roses
Enclose the hidden future:
Bleeding heart a sheaf of valentines,
Borage with its litmus-paper-mauve-
To-blue buds set in spiral,
Solomon's seal weighing the fateful options.

But now in winter, weltering snowfall downs
And downy snowdrift, banking up, blow through:
It's all one roofless chamber
Scored by branch and bole, a single upwards,
Single outwards gesture that composes
Heaven with blue horizon,
And watchman soul sees past the vanished walls
Windows opening on windows opening.

And so is Spinoza, in the adjacent fields, asserting that everything is God, and Benoit Mandelbrot, pointing out a great spray of fractals, and my friend Cinda Agnew Musters, who left for Holland more than fifty years ago but brought back (about twenty-five years ago) lots of tulips for the garden, some of which still come up. And my husband, still kicking the soccer ball around with the boys, reviving the 'beautiful game' that they discovered twenty years ago in England. So if that isn't a supernatural lapse of time in the woods behind my house, I don't know what is. There are always more poems under the trees, there and not there, confounding earth and heaven, bending the river of time around the great circles of the solar system, hatching in the debris that living things leave behind, sounding in the choir of the low plain chipmunks and the lofty bedazzled catholic birds.

Two Poems

RORY WATERMAN

Epithalamium

A Postscript for A.

He's in love with being in love
but how much love is left to give
at 78? She's 46,
Romanian, and here to live:

he's signed to her his full devotion
and terraced house. Now he sits
alone all day in a tiny room
he used to only sleep in. It's

a refuge. She sleeps where his office was
on a single mattress he acquired
then busies herself: this kitchen needs
stripping, then the yard. She's tired.

She fends off calls: 'No here, he sleepink'
she says a few times every day,
to grainy voices down the phone
who'd called to chat chess, poetry

or football, or later just to see
if anything might be done, or said.
She must negotiate, alone,
her GP, bank: he stays in bed.

And this is love – and then was love.
She grieves, sells up, then moves away
to where her folks can help; his son,
who only used to come to stay

when work allowed, won't bother her now.
Then one warm night she Google-translates
this poem, and smiles. Its subtleties
are more than she can navigate.

Reaping

'We need to test harder whether we can take a young 18- or 19-year-old out of their PlayStation bedroom, and put them into a Reaper cabin and say: "Right, you have never flown an aircraft before. That does not matter, you can operate this."'
— *Air Marshal Greg Bagwell*

18, 19 – what was I doing then?
Well, one day, I biked here
to RAF Waddington's 'viewing point',

from where I saw no action –
called by the urgent Tornados
which had fled across our village

shocking pliant heads
at intervals of my childhood,
and must have come from somewhere.

Runway approach lights have switched on
and point skywards at nothing
coming in. A pigeon. A slip of moon.

A screech owl would be too apposite.
But I saw one once a mile from here,
on Bloxholm Lane. It stalled a moment,

then beat on past the hedges
tall as houses, living its purpose
suddenly beyond range.

And who knows what they do
in a concreted cube two hundred yards
behind wires and warning signs,

or who does it – or why
an inch from where it would've died
a sandfly fills its nest?

Grasses by the road
dip like a million rods
to a million tiny catches. A saloon

half a mile off indicates
only to the clouding dusk,
slows to corner the perimeter

on a red route B road to home.
Nothing to do but follow
at a generous distance.

Two Poems

PETER ADAIR

The Acorn Road

That chilly morning a soldier dug a grave,
lowered down his mate and laid a wreath at the wall
of the garden. I stopped, too far off to see

if he wept, then pushed the wheelbarrow full
of acorns – thousands of acorns – to sow
in neat raised beds in a polytunnel.

Beyond the trees arose a general's chateau
behind their lines. I passed my great-uncle by chance
beside the willow cuttings in serried row

on row like gravestones in a field in France
forever Ulster. And creeping from tents
in Clandeboye, bricklayers, sons of the manse,

clerks, still in civvies, fired German rifles
at the birdie while gunshots resounded
in the woods – guests slaughtering partridges.

We buried the acorns, named the ridge Acorn Road,
as they might call their trenches homely names:
Sandy Row, Markethill: names spelt in blood.

Nearby, three lads sat at a rusty table
and played cards, chatted, as if they'd never left
this land. I walked over. We had so much to say,

so much, but the next moment they were lost
to sight, and the workless boy pushed a roller
over the Acorn Road to smooth the compost.

Later, I watched the soldiers march down darkened lanes
to another land, and gable murals on new estates.

Words

Words walk the streets searching for listeners.
Words talk to themselves, dribbling in their bibs.
Words forget how to spell and how to speak.
Words ask, 'How would we sound on someone's lips?'
Words are sentenced, paragraphed and shoved into a cell.
Words hunger-strike, grow beards, smear verbs on walls.
Words burn down the prison block and shoot the warders
Words are tasered, bound and bruised and dripping blood.
Words are stitched into straitjackets and roll on the floor.
Words are catatonic, curled up in heaps of noun corpses.

'While changing it rests'[1]
Gabriel Levin's *Coming Forth By Day*

PETER VERNON

IN PN REVIEW 243 I analysed the title poem of Gabriel Levin's *Coming Forth by Day*; here I concentrate on the final sequence: 'The Orphic Egg' where modern/post-modern concerns with high culture, self-reflexive media, the transitions, the impermanence of the contemporary world where everything is 'in motion', are brought into focus and given heightened tension. Levin here presents a vision of the power and significance of art; a vision that is expressed in the triple repetition of 'I thought I heard' which in the end becomes transformed into 'I thought I saw'. The power of the poem is found in the ekphrasis it creates from the music: 'but it all levels / out, down- and upbeat, in the pantonic hap'; or 'strive/ fall back, fuse, dissolve, good riddance to the dross'. These hammer-blows of spondees mimic Alexander Goehr's music, which inspired the poems. These are a series of five interlocking rondeaux, where the opening phrase of each poem operates as a burden or refrain, repeated as a half-line at lines 9 and 15, which, since there is no end stop to the stanza, then lead into the opening of the next rondeau. Thus, the first line of stanza 1 reads: 'Ever in motion, rest assured, [...]', the opening phrase 'Ever in motion' becomes line 9, and is repeated at the end of the stanza at line 15 which thus introduces line 1 of the next rondeau: 'won't you tell us the score'. Such a repetitive structure, like a theme and variations, is taken from music as the name 'rondeau' suggests, and the form is perfectly adapted to reflect Goehr's music. The rondeau is a complex form, but the repetitions enable easy oral transmission; the structure reflects the music, and leads beyond words to a vision of transcendent creativity. Levin's poem is, from the opening lines, full of alliteration and oxymoron: 'Ever in motion, rest assured'. The music is continuous, and like the sea, it is 'ever in motion'; we can 'rest assured' i.e. be certain, but we can also be assured of 'rest' in terms of repose, and 'rest' as remainder, while 'rest' in music or prosody is a pause or caesura exemplified in the opening line, 'Ever in motion, rest assured' (evident tension is generated by the oxymoron found in 'motion' juxtaposed with 'rest'). 'Rest assured' is transformed at line 10 into 'rest your case', where the flautist rests his case in the sense of 'proven or completed argument' and the plosives found in 'pulling fissures', 'employ / in the plying' mirror the puckered lips of the player. The form of Levin's sequence of rondeaux is appropriated from Sir Thomas Wyatt.[2] Two quotations will make the case of debt and difference more efficiently than any descriptive analysis; here is Wyatt's 'Rondeau' No. 17:

Help me to seek, for I lost it there,
And if that ye have found it, ye that be here,
And seek to convey it secretly,
Handle it soft and treat it tenderly,
Or else it will be plain and then appear:

But rather restore it mannerly,
Since that I do ask it thus honestly:
For to lose it, it sitteth me too near.
Help me to seek.

Alas, and is there no remedy?
But I have thus lost it wilfully?
Iwis it was a thing all too dear
To be bestowed and wist not where:
It was my heart, I pray you heartily
Help me to seek. (*Silver Poets*, 8)

In contrast, here is the second rondeau in Levin's sequence:

won't you tell us the score? Before
　　we disperse, won't you guide us to the shore
the lucent strand? *While changing it rests*
　　was how I heard the heaved from the chest
melodic line, the variable foot, with more

　　in store for the untutored guest
for whom song was the Orphic Egg, the quest
　　launched in water and mud, in cryptic lore
　　　　won't you tell us

the score? Time the serpent, and all the rest
　　the unravelling coreless beat, the behest
that begets, the gap that drills a hole in fore-
　　thought, briefly take the floor
restore the measure, the momentary blest
　　　　won't you tell us
(63–64)

In Wyatt's rondeau the sections are end-stopped and he employs caesural pauses with internal rhyme and many monosyllabic repetitions ('be', 'ye', 'it' etc.) and the poem is structured around the search for 'it', his heart, which he has lost, and hopes his lover will find. There are some archaisms 'sitteth' meaning suits or fits; 'Iwis' (Ywis) meaning certainly; 'wist' meaning knew. Wyatt's rondeau is obviously accomplished; it plays wittily with the traditional tropes of losing one's heart and, because of this, reads something like an exercise in courtly poetry. In comparison, Levin's poem presents greater challenges. In part, this is because it is composed of a sequence of rondeaux with an added 'Coda', so the poem gathers increasingly complex significance as it develops. But the real challenge emerges when we consider how the poem is unified with the music that inspired it; in Levin's poem we are not simply looking for a lost heart, we are probing the meaning of existence. This is no exercise, but rather a meditation on what music can represent. For such a theme it is fitting that the poem is full of musical terms ('rest', 'fingers stops', 'melodic line', 'song', 'score', 'cadenza', 'measure', 'coda' etc.). The vocabulary switches rapidly from Anglo-Saxon 'behest', 'beget', to Graeco-Latin 'sidereal', 'pantonic'. His frequent paradox and oxymoron, line breaks, and idioms, gather further significance, making interpretation more problematic. The lines: 'ever in motion // won't you tell us the score' exemplify the problems of interpretation, where 'tell us the score' signifies so much more than tell us 'what's happening'; it asks how the musical score presents itself, how *can* the music be incarnated? Portraying himself as 'the untutored guest', Levin struggles to find words to express the music, and in the penultimate rondeau writes: 'the hard drive/ circuitry of technique I'd be at a loss// to follow'. Like Wyatt, Levin employs frequent internal rhyme, binding the poem together, 'the behest / that begets', but his imagery is, like the music, in constant motion. 'Time', in the second rondeau, is a serpent, whilst in the final poem the image is transposed 'into the swirl, in no time sidereal, I thought / I heard a serpentine piping wrought' (65).

The title 'The Orphic Egg' confronts us with the Orphic mystery of Phanes/Protogonos (the Revealer/ First Born) a hermaphroditic sun deity who sprang from the silver egg encircled by a serpent from which the entire universe was created. An Orphic hymn describes Phanes: 'Ineffable, hidden, brilliant scion, whose motion is whirring, you scattered the dark mist that lay before your eyes and, flapping your wings, you whirled about, and through this world you brought pure light' ('To Protogonos'). 'The Orphic Egg', then, may be seen as a meditation upon artistic creativity, the creator as 'Phanes / Revealer'; the Latin equivalent would be 'Vates', a diviner, one who descends into the darkness of self, and brings the quick stuff of feeling into light. The figure is peculiarly apt for Levin, because his poetry reveals from the depths, and fuses old and new. His verse is created from an auditory imagination, defined by Eliot as 'the feeling for syllable and rhythm, penetrating far below the conscious levels of thought and feeling, invigorating every word; sinking to the most primitive and forgotten, returning to the origin and bringing something back, seeking the beginning and the end' (Eliot, 118–19). Levin in this sequence has put his reader back in touch with creative mystery and with birth and light. In addition to the musical imagery, he adds a further level of elemental imagery: 'water and mud', 'air streams', and, as befits Phanes the sun deity, there is a predominance of light and fire imagery: 'lucent', 'combustion', 'hail and fire', 'crackling flames', 'resplendent'.

Whilst all is in motion, yet art remains and this concluding poem is enriched by the words (Levin's translation printed in italics within the poem) of the first Jewish Vizier of Berber Andalucia, Shmuel HaNagid (993–1056), whose name translates as 'Samuel the Prince'. Although Jewish, Shmuel led the armies of Granada into battle, and achieved the highest rank in Andalucia (Carmi, 98). Levin quotes from Shmuel's 'Winter Wine Song', which, together with the music of Alexander Goehr, inspires Levin to his very finest poetry, as he connects back to his own poetic roots and takes a visionary step into the future:

I thought I heard companions long dormant

calling, *Let each man pitch all he's got*
                                        into the swirl

in no time real as anything off the reel, advent
    or egress, I thought I saw ascendant
shorn free, the body politic as a translucent dot
    a minim field no longer fraught
by daily cumbrances, borne up resplendent
                                        into the swirl (65)

This is a vision of 'New Jerusalem', not descending like St John's 'bride adorned for her husband' (Rev. 21, 2), but re-written in the Real in the potential force of a communion of poets and artists throughout history; a vision of New Jerusalem now *ascending* into a creative vortex as prefigured by Blake and Lawrence, although the music and tension in the words may also be compared to Hopkins. And, in the final 'Coda' to 'The Orphic Egg', the writing is the music is the orphic egg, which is about to hatch and give birth to the living universe in the figure of Phanes, first-born from the egg:

a diabolic piping of the acutest
measure, sparking the spark lying
ready to spark where the serpent flickers
its tongue, and it is good, *Hwaet!* (66)

The Anglo-Saxon 'Hwaet' employed here, in the context of Orphic myth, connects narratives and myths from Mediterranean culture with our own Early English legends and exemplifies yet again the cosmopolitan aspects of Levin's poetry.

What confronts, challenges and enchants the reader of this collection is the play of Levin's words. One emerges from reading these poems with an appreciation of his restless curiosity, his exceptionally keen observation and concentration, his practical imagination, which plays powerfully upon the reader, and demands of him a considered judgement. Levin is not an easy poet; perhaps no good contemporary poet can be, but it is more than that. Seamus Heaney's words on Eliot may apply equally to Levin, for he shows: 'how poetic vocation entails the disciplining of a habit of expression until it becomes fundamental to the whole conduct of a life' (Heaney, 38). Levin is a fine poet who asks fundamental questions of himself and his readers, in a complicity of mutual creativity, which, if worked for, gives a final, hard-won message of hope in the transforming power of poetry and art: he deserves a very wide readership.

NOTES
1   'It is in changing that things find repose' (Haraclitus, Frag. 23), Levin adapts this fragment in 'The Orphic Egg' (63): '*While changing it rests / was how I heard the heaved from the chest / melodic line, the variable foot...*'
2   Oral transmission, solicited by the repetitive structure, is reinforced by brace rhyme schemes of the rondeaux, with the third rhyme (C) located at lines 9 and 15. Wyatt uses various rhyme schemes, while Levin's 'The Orphic Egg' borrows the pattern from Wyatt's No. 17: AABBA/ BBAC / BBAABC. (The best definition of 'rondeaux' will be found in *Princeton*, 1097–8).

'Let me Explain' and other poems

Au Secours

An Earl in a red bush.
A pearl in the ointment.
A pig in clover.

The mountain and the valley folds.
The rabbit ear also
but an ear for what?

For reasonable adjustments
and no mistake.

Let me explain:

'*C'est monstrueux*', says Eugène Ionesco,
using a rather nice walking stick to denounce
the whole of the London scene before him.

And not just London – he means everything.

The inscription on his tomb in Montparnasse
      cemetery reads:

Prier-le Je Ne Sais Qui
J'espère : Jesus-Christ.

Pray to the I don't-know-who:
Jesus Christ, I hope.

Meaning what and for whom?

For snowfall. That's fatal.
A heavy dew even.

We're all undone
in the long run
eat peaches, play cricket
on the floor
about the door
              handles and windows
        falling off
            whatever kind of guarantee
we might ever have had

6.28 a.m.   Quiet birds   spin cycle

And now here's H in my dressing gown
and his Christmas angel's singing in high heels
by my shoulder
while I'm dressing down for Gertrude
giving us what, a cold meat selection?

Good morning Finn

May you be happy
in green sunshine
heavy dew ham and eggs

Some Additional Information

/ˈɪəuː// ˈiːuː/
- 'They loaded me up with hape and pale pink lipstick.'
- 'I'll miss the dirty look he wpy gas, told me I had an abscess (eww), drilled out some decay and took $200 out of my pocke'ed O
- This selection of peep-toe boots, hpeared at first.'
- 'She wasn't even that pretty wiww' faxfords and stud of high school in my public school career and I've got to study for finals... eww!w'
- en on my feet (eww) sometimes.'ded short boots (I'm sorry, Ggets that particular beat... eww.'lue ey lemon. ewt.'ctor is higc6 more days
- She looks like a baked dancing then I feel like eww you're just staring at my boobs.'ape I have
- 'An "eww" from the children caused'They're funny because y brother.'th ssible sincher cont them to part and laugh.'men h of
- We wouldn't like to be the s see the ligh
- 'Big hair and pencil skirts (eww) ked me out bect?'the "e
- ctucci, but eww) should notlled Tanner ts, eww Kasha wannabould give you whday.' face aause at first I'ma what has been trampled into that carpet'ly makes her scarier when she turns on Christine.'
- 'Oh eww I just catreet clee yawned in your'I w
- 'eww, how can you eat thaner who b'But that's also no'ew,n adding in, the ' eww... boys have cooties ' years.'t poigh-heel'It sinkyou went "eww!"'
- 'One glove was... eww... in the t
- w I'd hate to thih, but that on other wish I was as tough as the ski'Yeah, I'm eveith that disgusting old dog breath, and oilet, and theas filthy.'

'Lobsters, Americans' and other poems

SUZANNAH V. EVANS

Silk, Poets

Silk coat, the sky.
Sky blue, the creels.
Crawling, the lobsters.
Leaping, the mackerel.
Making, the poets.
Peering, the tourists.
Tipping, the waves.
Waving, the poets.
Pining, the lovers.
Lullabying, the dreamers.
Dreaming, the sleepers.
Swimming, the brave,
Braving, the poets.

Still Life With Five Starfish, Two Razor Shells, a Twig, a Clam and a Frond of Seaweed

Five starfish, as if one for each arm. A symmetry.
The shell is so white against the black-struck sand,
almost spotless (only a flicker of sediment near its
jewellery-box hinge: o -----).
Next to it, a sand-coloured starfish: *
Adjacent again, a bright white starfish: *
next to a bright white razor shell: <-----------> (or rather, half),
itself next to a larger razor shell (the image too explicit, legs opened)
stretched white, glimmering. A dream of salt.
The pages of a book. Other starfish merge with the sand: ***
arms tangled in an intimacy of seaweed.
And that frond of seaweed: ~- - ~--- ~ ~ --- ~ ~,
laid out by the sea like a bookmark,
like the sea marking its place in the order of things.

Lobsters, Americans

Lobster pots in gardens, cackling gulls (a
chick begging for food, catching the beak of its mother)
roll of suitcases over the cobbles, *caw-caw-ha-ha-mouette*
-mouette-mouette of seagulls in the air, mustard trousers
a couple holding hands, two gulls above them
scent of brine, scent of lobsters
cobbles   rope   twine
salt on the tongue, on the tonsils
a boat, tied, that moves in its moorings as if it has caught
a holy spirit and must express the spirit though leanings, shiftings
the boats are all still, the boats are all moving
white mist, white gulls   white on the breeze
stone   stone   stone   stone   stone   stone
cigarette butts on the ground, stairs leading to doors
men talking seriously, twine in their fingers
the rattle of car keys offsetting the gulls
and a conversation between Americans   rising

Coilings

ropes coil like eels (eelish the ropes, creelish the creels)
and conversations between Americans disturb the mist
(a dog runs on the beach, a smaller sits to the side of my vision)
a castle, a cathedral: it's a vision, curling, coiling (mist, creel)

a surfer, swimming, and my hands sting with cold
as I write, curled, coiled, eeled, on the bench, dreaming, (dr)eeling,
listening to the silent conversation of fishermen as they twine
and drink tea (as brown as the brown sea tossing on the strand)

rope – flags – grit – creels – eels – mackerel – crates – tyres – boats
(the sea makes its own waves, sloshing itself over the earth)
the sea coils blue waves up up up into the air, breathing

creels, tumbled together
eels, coiled
rope, oiled

Lobster Creels

The lobster creels are victoriously blue,
shining, letting through the light (dim) of the sky:
oh so blue, the sky would be, if it were not misted,
if it was not a silk grey coat for the lovers who walk on the pier.

The pier is a long thought, stretched into the sea.
The sea is many thoughts, fragmented and sifted
by some other consciousness. The creels are nets for thoughts.
The fishermen voice thoughts into the cool March air.

The stones are harbours for thoughts, soaking up salt,
soaking up the ash of conversations between lovers,
between hurrying students. The harbour is a harbour for boats.
The chimney pots are resting places for birds and lofty thoughts.

An attic room is good to think in, an attic room is good
to shower and stretch in, to sluice off sand in.
An attic room is a page for poetry, is a glance into the sky.
Oh so silk, the sky is, unravelling into the night.

Madame de Sévigné Writes to Her Daughter

SAM ADAMS

Paris, February 1671

I am waiting. I haven't any news from you –
nothing of your journey to Lyon and on into Provence.
No doubt you have written; no doubt a letter
will come. While I wait, I console and amuse myself
writing to you.

At three this morning I was awakened by cries:
Fire! Fire! And rising in haste and fear saw the house
of Guitaud alight, flames rising above the roofs
of neighbouring houses, confusion everywhere,
a terrible crashing of falling beams, and Guitaud,
steeled to plunge into the inferno to rescue his mother
on the third floor, struggling to free himself
from his wife's grasp, and she five months' pregnant.
When he found his mother was safe,
still he fought to retrieve some precious papers,
but couldn't get near for the heat. At last,
about five, we thought of his wife's delicate condition.
We had her bled, but still we feared she might go into labour.

If one could have laughed on such a sad occasion,
what pictures one could paint of the state we were all in:
Guitaud naked but for nightshirt and shoes, his wife
bare-legged, one foot slipperless; Madame Vauvineux
in short skirt without her negligée; everyone, servants
and all, wearing nightcaps. Thankfully, the Ambassador
from Venice with dressing-gown and wig, sustained
the gravity of *la serenissima*. But his secretary
was altogether admirable. You speak of the breast
of Hercules, well she was something else!
White and chubby, and above all without even a chemise,
having lost in the fray the cord to secure it.

As for me, though full of pity for my poor neighbours,
I felt somehow detached. There you are –
the news from our quarter. I have told our butler
to do the rounds every night and make sure
all fires are out. You can't be too careful.

My dear child, I think only of you. No one
is more dearly loved than you are by me. I pray
you are never bored by this repetition of my love.

Paris, February 1674

Nothing would please me more than to take up
my pen every day. Whenever I can
I jot a line or two, even if, in the end,
I don't send the letter. What matters is I am writing
just for you, my dearest daughter. For the rest of the world
I write only because I must.

The Archbishop of Reims returned yesterday
like a whirlwind. He fancies himself
a great lord, and his people think him so, too.
They thundered through Nanterre –
tra, tra, tra – and met a man on horseback
coming the other way: *Gare! Gare! Gare!*
The man hauled on the reins and the horse
didn't budge, so that both tumbled hirdie-girdie
under the wheels of the carriage and six
and almost toppled it. By some miracle
man and horse rose together, the one
mounted the other and they galloped off,
while Archbishop, coachman and lackeys
bawled, *Stop him – Stop that villain.*
If I had caught him, the Archbishop said,
I'd have broken his arms and cut off his ears.

Adieu my dearest, my lovely one. Never fear
my delight in you will fade. I think only
of the joy I shall feel in embracing you soon.

Aux Rochers, September 1675

I write to you, my dearest, from all the places I can,
while neglected friends may think I have
drowned in the Loire.

I left la Silleraye yesterday and arrived
earlier today, to find Mlle du Plessis more
frightful, mad and impertinent than ever.
Her regard for me does me no honour. On my oath,
I have never by any show of kindness or friendship
earned her approbation. I say the most abominable
things to her – she thinks them all in jest; I try
to ignore her – it doesn't stop her hanging round me.

The woods here have an extraordinary beauty,
and sadness. All the trees you knew when you were small
have since grown tall and perfectly beautiful. They spread
about them the pleasantest shade. I feel a kind of maternal
love for them, having planted them all and seen them –
as M. de Montbazon says, *no bigger than that.*
Here is solitude made for reverie. You would enjoy it
and I don't regret it, so long as the thoughts that come
are not black, or at least no more than grey
or brown. I think of you all the time. I miss you
and wish you may be well, and that your affairs
prosper. This verse runs round inside my head:
    What cruel star dictates from above
    This unconscionable distance from my love.

Paris, July 1676

My dear, dear child, here I am to my heart's content,
alone in my room, writing to you. Nothing pleases me more
for I love you beyond all things.

Madame de Brinvilliers, in prison, asked for a partner
to play piquet, because she was bored. She confessed
that she poisoned her father, her brothers, one of her children
and herself, but only to test an antidote. Medea did less!
She agreed the confession was by her own hand,
but it was all nonsense; she was in a fever at the time –
it was delirium, a joke, not to be taken seriously.

And now it's done. La Brinvilliers is aloft,
mingled with the air. Her pathetic corpse
tossed on a huge fire and the ashes cast to the winds.
We breathed something of that poison that astonished all of us.

She was condemned yesterday, and the judgement
proclaimed this morning – beheading, her body to be burned,
her dust scattered. She said nothing,
having said enough already. Life had become more unbearable
than she ever could have dreamed. She had dosed her father
with poison ten times, unable to stop herself – and so her brothers,
all with the same mingling of solicitude and love.

At six o'clock she was led out, naked but for a shift,
a noose about her neck, to Notre Dame to make
her quittance. There I saw her thrown back on the straw
in the tumbril, in her shift, a little horned cap on her head,
a doctor on one side, the executioner on the other.
It was a sight to make you tremble. They say
she mounted the scaffold with no sign of fear.
I stayed on the bridge by Notre Dame;
if you were to ask what most of that great crowd
saw, I would say no more than I – the horned cap on her head.

Our little friend, Madame de Coulanges,
made me laugh this morning. She said Madame de Rochefort
has always cherished the most exquisite feelings
for Madame de Montespan, and she pretended to sob
and sigh while telling me how de Rochefort
adored that beauty. Are you naughty enough
to find this as amusing as I do?

Adieu, my dear child, I embrace you a thousand times
with a tenderness beyond words.

After Rubix

KATHERINE LOCKTON

Red:

'Look how he steps on birds' wings' they say,
'how he grabs at their feathers and makes
them his. If he falls it will be onto their backs'.

'We don't know our own bodies. I feel for my
thigh and find your calf, then her hip and his nose.
My thigh is lost somewhere between our bodies.'

They put him in a house too small for him.
Its walls push against his ears. This is
what they had said would happen if he lied.

What red does:

Our aunt sits us on giant chairs and tells us to stay.
We mustn't, we shouldn't, we can't and if we do.
The tomatoes sit on their shelf untouched but bruised.

We push him in a pram too big for us to hold,
our arms grabbing only the wheels. This is what
it is to love my mother tells us; to push and push.

He doesn't know why he leans on this gate so much.
He only knows he fed the chickens here once, his
feet thick with mud. Sandra, his wife, calling calling.

What our parents don't say about red:

They painted bits of themselves red just to
feel the paint against them. It peeled off that very
night but they had felt what it was to be free.

When they no longer had a use for Miss X, they
turned her into a bike; her rear became a seat;
her neck; handles; fitted wheels onto her calves.

They planted us head down, stuck us as deep
as their hands could carve into mud and rock.
They didn't know we were weeds.

Yellow:

We bloomed in that nightly silence, danced
in its darkness. When they lit that match,
we had no use for that yellow beam.

The redness of their dance was all
we felt. Their blurred bodies moving
and moving until all we felt was them.

She threaded stones into her corset till
she could no longer move and waited.
The potatoes turned green on their shelves.

What yellow does:

It lay on its belly, broken. The world
seemed bathed in white light. The only one
of its kind made like this – made to break.

The day they wed, her mum threw birdseed
at their heads for luck. When the seed fell
nearby pigeons came; eyes wide with hunger.

They hung the foal's mother, her head bowed;
as if she somehow knew to stay silent.
The men stood around in batches pointing.

Blue:

We cover our breasts in bees. The yellow
of them comforts us. They sting as they
try to suckle milk that was never meant for them.

With blunt scissors she chops away at the part of her
that loves him still. Her hair gone,
she contemplates cutting away at the rest.

While waiting for him to come home, she lays
out herself the way others lay out linen.
Her arms, legs, chest all neatly folded.

What our parents don't say
about blue:

To cigarette in the city is to laugh, mouth wide
with candy: to stare into your loved one's
eyes as they smooth you down.

Her shadow still shows the missing bits of her.
The ones she put in the washing machine
just to be rid of the smell of herself.

He puts himself into a bottle for her. At six foot
two his feet stick out. The way they always did
in bed. She uses his shoes to push him down.

What our parents don't say
about yellow:

The newborn bairns are in cots lined up
against blue walls, hello kitties painted
onto their feet. Outside it is raining still.

They are wearing huge glittery condoms
on their skulls and walking across fifth avenue
like this. They are praying, they say.

She blows bubbles as big as wild bears,
dancing to music only she hears. This time, this time,
they will take her away her neighbours say.

What blue does:

When I find that one of me is not enough.
I print eleven other versions just to
see if any number of me will ever be.

Our mother won't let us play with the neighborhood
squirrels. Their fur is too thick, their legs
too thin. So she sends us to the sea.

The pigeons steal the newly wed couple
in their sleep, take them above clouds
never meant for the young and drop them.

A Translator's Notebook (10)

From Budapest to Glasgow

EDWIN MORGAN

edited by James McGonigal

EDWIN MORGAN *usually kept a pocket notebook when he went on poetry-reading or lecture tours abroad. Here he jotted down details of flights and train journeys, meals, encounters and street observations – maximum information in miniscule handwriting. All these notebooks are archived in Glasgow University Library's Special Collections (MS Morgan H.). The one that Morgan kept in the autumn of 1966, when he and poet and BBC radio producer George MacBeth were members of a British Council group attending an international poetry congress in Budapest, has claims to be a real translator's notebook, since he attended on the strength of his work in East European translation. It was not a very comfortable first week, with a packed schedule of conference papers to be listened to either in Russian, Hungarian or 'broken French'. In the second week he gave a paper on translation and lectured on modern British poetry at Budapest University and the British Embassy: 'I slipped some (phonic) concrete into my lectures and caused something of a sensation,' he reported to Robert Tait, soon to be his co-editor on* Scottish International *journal.*

More significant, however, were opportunities to meet Hungarian poets such as Ottó Orbán and Sándor Weöres, and also Miklós Vajda, literary editor of the New Hungarian Quarterly [NHQ]. *The latter would have noted Morgan's translations of seven poems by Attila József in the Budapest magazine* Arion *earlier that year, as well as of Lajos Kassák and János Pilinszky in* NHQ VII: 23. *He told Morgan that he had a good touch in translating Hungarian poets, and arranged to send him rough English translations of poems for him to work on – the start of a fruitful collaboration with the journal.*

But the meeting with Sándor Weöres was of a different order, and made a life-long impression. Morgan's notebook pages describe their meal in an old and atmospheric literary café, with 'instant poems and drawings exchanged multilingually and concretely between Weöres and myself'. Weöres spoke no English, though his wife did, but knew some French and Russian. He seemed to Morgan then 'an extraordinary man – small, puckered face, young-looking though about 50, great sense of fun (hence concrete and phonic poems). [...] Contrast between utterly dead official public conference and lively warm personal contact so extreme.' They met again a day or so later, and discussed the possibility of translating his poetry, although he had no spare copies of his works to give to Morgan.

Recalling in his early eighties their brief encounters in Budapest, Morgan still seems to sparkle with enthusiasm and admiration:

He knew, he surely knew what he was: I think he was a genius. He knew he was a great poet and therefore ought to be known in the English language. [...] He had, of course, a humorous impish quality, which was very attractive – almost a kind of child-like quality. He would think of something quite entertaining, quite funny, and just say it, even though it had no tremendous depth to it. I liked that about him: there was a kind of innocence perhaps.

Those who knew Morgan will recognise some of those same qualities in him, although he himself perhaps would not have owned to innocence. There was also in Weöres a spiritual depth and complexity very different to the values Morgan had developed through a Scottish upbringing. But both men shared interests in mythology, anthropology, aesthetics, the translation of Ukrainian poetry, epic poetry and a thousand other topics: 'I liked the way the conversation flew very freely back and forward. There were a great variety of subjects: nothing was taboo, or difficult or awkward, it just flew very naturally.'

(This interview with Attila Dósa is in Beyond Identity: New Horizons in Modern Scottish Poetry, *ed. A. Dósa. Amsterdam: Rodopi, 2009: 35–57.)*

In the year following this Budapest visit, Morgan's translation of Hungarian poetry intensified, to judge from the regular appearance of his work in NHQ *– István Kormos in VIII: 25, Spring 1967, Zoltán Jékeli in VIII: 26, Summer 1967, and Sándor Csoóri in VIII: 27, Autumn. None of these poets appears in* Collected Translations *1996 [CT]. Presumably Morgan was responding to Vajda's drafts, although I've found no trace of these: he disliked keeping notes or drafts alongside holograph poems. He was also preparing a talk on Modern Hungarian Poetry for the BBC Third Programme, which was broadcast on 14 March 1968, and reprinted in a slightly abridged version in* NHQ *IX: 31, 143–61, Autumn 1968. I am going to abridge this talk further here and concentrate only on his remarks about Attila József and Sándor Weöres, omitting László Nagy and Ferenc Juhász, neither of whom were collected in CT. In the broadcast he uses his own translations of József, described as being by an unnamed contemporary 'English' poet, but he makes some pointed remarks about the free translations of Weöres by other named contemporaries, and I'd like to illustrate by contrast the different effects that he himself was seeking.*

* * *

EDWIN MORGAN, 'MODERN HUNGARIAN POETRY'

Poetry in Hungary in the twentieth century has been as striking and varied as it has anywhere else in Europe, but with the barrier of the Hungarian language and the difficulties of translation it has taken longer for a knowledge of this achievement to filter through to the West. The Hungarians are all the more acutely aware of the neglected values of their poetry because these values, although they're national and irreplaceable in the sense of being rooted in Hungarian language and Hungarian history and culture, are far from parochial: the very isolation of their non-Indo-European tongue forces the Hungarians to become linguists and translators and to study and assimilate the range of European poetic achievement on a scale that is quite unfamiliar to poets in the English-speaking world. Symbolism and expressionism, futurism and surrealism and several sorts of imagism have all left their mark on Hungarian poetry, to say nothing of the Central and Eastern European traditions of political and historical involvement, yet the final result is not a hotchpotch of extraneous fashions. Something strong and distinctive inheres natively and transforms the foreign influences into its own articulations. In fact it would be surprising if this failed to happen, since poetry is a great instrument of national identity, and the history of Hungary under its invaders and oppressors from east and west is the dogged persistence of an entity, small, unique, islanded, self-aware.

The lyrical, epic, patriotic or prophetic poetry of the nineteenth century established a national tradition in the works of Petőfi, Vörösmarty and Arany. In the modern period, Hungarian interest in the symbolist and post-symbolist poetry of the West, as well as in the folk-resources of their own poetry and language, has produced a rich and often complex and difficult poetic art. I have picked out four poets to represent something of the scope of this twentieth-century poetry. Many other names would be required for a complete picture, but I think the chosen writers will suggest some of the main preoccupations and qualities of the period. The selection of poems depended on the translations that were available, and in each case I've used versions made by contemporary English poets – fairly free versions by Peter Redgrove and George MacBeth.

One of the best Hungarian poets, of any period, is Attila József, who was born into a poor family in 1905, and died at his own hand in 1937. After a number of temporary jobs, such as a ship's boy on a Danube steamer, railway porter, street peddler, he had a spell at the University of Szeged, but was expelled for subversive writing. He went abroad for a while, to Vienna and Paris, became interested in the poetry of Apollinaire, in German expressionism, in the ideas of Freud and Marx. He came back to devote his energy to the development and revitalisation of his native poetic traditions. His greatest poetry belongs to the disturbed years of the 1930s, it reflects oppression and poverty, and foreboding, and also social hope and prophecy. Its imagery is very striking, and it gives a strong sense of personal involvement.

The first of the poems that I'd like you to hear is very typical of the urban theme that József made so much of. The city and its outskirts, the alienated industrial landscape, were focal points both for his wonderful sense of atmosphere and for his feeling that here society itself shows the face of its time, the horror of economic or political servitude, and yet it is also the place of protest and brotherhood and hope. Here then is 'Night in the Suburbs':

[Editor: Morgan then reads the whole poem, too long to quote more than a few stanzas here to reveal his use of half-rhyme and assonance. The poem is in Collected Translations [CT] 1996: 360–2]

The light smoothly withdraws
its net from the yard, and as water
gathers in the hollow of the ditch,
darkness has filled our kitchen.

Silence – The scrubbing-brush sluggishly
rises and drags itself about;
above it, a small piece of wall is in
two minds to fall or not.

The greasy rags of the sky
have caught the night; it sighs;
it settles down on the outskirts;
it sets off through the square, going where?
It kindles a dim moon for a fire

Attila József also wrote more intimate, personal poetry, and the following short poem 'Mother' is a famous example of it:

All this last week I have been thinking
of my mother, thinking of her taking
up in her arms the creaking basket
of clothes, without pausing, up to the attic.

Oh I was full of myself in those days –
shouting and stamping, crying to her to leave
her washing to others, to take me in place
of the basket, play with me under the eaves –

But calmly she went on, lifting out the clothes,
hanging them to dry, she had no time to scold
or even to glance at me, and soon the line
was flying in the wind, white and clean.

I cannot shout now – how could she hear?
I see her, great, vast, yet somehow she is near.
The wet sky shines washed with her blue,
her grey hair streams where the clouds scud through.
    [CT: 341–2]
[Editor: The reference in the penultimate line is to 'washing blue' or 'dolly blue', a synthetic dye that used to be added to white laundry to enhance brightness.]

In some poems József made use of ballad forms in a way rather reminiscent of Brecht. Here is an ironic example, with repeated lines within the stanza and also a refrain-line linking one stanza to the next. It's called 'Keep Going!':

Mandarins hanged in Peking,
the dead man liked his cocaine.
– Go to sleep, you're rustling the straw.
The dead man liked his cocaine.

What does the poor man watch
through the window? Till and cash.
– Go to sleep, you're rustling the straw.
Through the window? Till and cash.

Buy yourself sausage and bread,
keep hardy, keep your head.
– Go to sleep, you're rustling the straw.
Keep hardy, keep your head.

You'll find the woman of gold,
she'll cook and never scold.
– Go to sleep, you're rustling the straw.
She'll cook and never scold.
    [CT: 343–4]

One of József's last poems attempts to combine historical and personal themes. The menacing world-war preludes of the thirties in Spain and China throw huge shadows over a human love-affair, and the poem finally tips the balance against pessimism by a visionary glance into a more distant future. Here is 'March 1937':

[Editor: There is space here only for the first, second and fifth stanzas of this poem, available in CT: 355–6.]

Soft rain is drifting like a smoke
across the tender fuzz of wheat.
As soon as the first stork appears
winter shrivels in retreat.
Spring comes, tunneling a path
mined with exploding spikes of green.
The hut, wide open to the sun
breathes hope and wood-dust sharp and clean.

The papers say that mercenaries
are ravaging the face of Spain.
A brainless general in China
chases peasants from hill to plain.
The cloth we use to wipe our boots
comes laundered back in blood again.
All round, big words bemuse and smooth
the voiceless miseries of men.
[...]
May our daughter be beautiful
and good, our son be fearless, keen.
May they transmit some sparks beyond
star-clusters you and I have seen.
When this sun loses its great fire,
the children of our illumination
will launch towards infinity
their own galactic exploration. [CT: 355–6]

Probably the most original, most individual poet now writing in Hungary is Sándor Weöres, who was born into a family of small landowners in Western Hungary in 1913. He studied law, history, geography, and philosophy at the universities of Pécs and Budapest, and has worked as a librarian, literary editor and translator. He is a virtuoso in every technical aspect of poetry, and his verse translations, which aim at reproducing even word-play and sound-effects, must be among the most remarkable ever made. His own poetry ranges from solitary, brooding meditations, through a wide range of mythological fantasy to nursery rhymes and 'concrete' poems which make use of both typographical and phonetic effects. Humour and playfulness and childlike wonder alternate with deep metaphysical analysis and an ingrained, Blakean sense of alienation from material reality. His chief collections are *The Tower of Silence* (1956) and *Well of Flames* (1964).

Of the three poems I want to use to illustrate Weöres's work, the first is a characteristically oblique short poem called 'Landscape with Mountain'. The disarmingly conventional title conceals an almost sinister awe. The translations of Weöres are by Peter Redgrove:

In the valley: ever-rumple of brook,
And ever-rustle of bird-voices.

Above: silence hangs
Where rocks reign. Rock-face;

God-face.
Higher still and very high, assuredly nobody sings.
At the very top: grindstone-screech,
Ice crackling headpiece.

*

Next, an extract from a long poem called 'Queen Tatavane'. Weöres has always been interested in myth and legend and particularly in pantheistic, transnational conceptions of nature. As far as possible from the intense social reality and social indignation of József, his intimations of a larger and non-human life seen through primitive eyes link him back to *The Golden Bough* and forward to structuralist anthropology. In this poem the ambiguous quality of myth, at once life-giving and inhibiting, emerges through a profusion of sensuous symbols:

QUEEN TATAVANE
Oh, you were winged, you ancestors!
You gave me green bough springing
And dry twig splintering
So that I could plant, beat two empires.
I am neat as a weasel,
Virgin as Diana's bow,
My ankle is the gazelle's though I do not flee,
My heart drumming watches for your silent advice.

My fifteenth year went into the maw of the Elephantstar.
The Dragonstar conceived this sixteenth.
My ancestors permit my three husbands,
My seven lovers under the jasmine-boughs.

I am not a girl like the others
That love to glide through the meadows,
Laugh into their sleeves,
Milk goats and drink the sweet milk.
Instead I am enthroned in your light year after year,
And the burden of the world is on my head.
It is an ebony idol.

Negro caravans and Arabian ships; I buy and sell.
They are all polecats, stinking, or stinking monkeys,
But I reward well.
I am the sky that is not troubled
Where its showers fall
Or what will spring
From the simmering earth,
Only that it is simmering.

There is the naked herd of the condemned.
I am their father and their mother.
I chastise them with rods,
And if needful, the sword.
I watch the heads bounding
And if I bleed in my heart
These tearducts are ignorant.

[Editor: These are the first four of twelve broadcast stanzas.]

And finally, here is Sándor Weöres in lighter vein, slightly surreal; a variation on Caesar's dislike of Cassius. It is called 'Antithin':

At last it has leaked out – thin men are the cause of everything.
They wait in ambush on street corners and if an old woman goes by
they don't ever greet her. They are more concerned with exchanging their
straw hats for lottery tickets, and with naturalising crocodiles in

the waters of Europe, so that even here there should be no safety.
They always begin their fishy deals in their beds at dawn, and
afterwards go to the street. Some work in offices, others ostensibly
are waiters or locksmiths – they all disguise themselves. But their
true trade is thinness. At last it has leaked out – thin men are, etc.
[Transl. by Richard Lourie]

* * *

At this point, Morgan moves on to László Nagy and Ferenc Juhász, neither of whom is in CT. *The latter, translated by David Wevill, is paired with Morgan's Weöres translations in a Penguin Modern European Poets in Translation volume (1970). His Introduction to that Penguin selection is reprinted in* CT. *Originally this was to have been a József–Weöres volume, with Peter Redgrove as the already chosen translator of Weöres. But seeing the quality of Morgan's translations he firstly entered into partnership with him and then withdrew. Something of that story is told in* Beyond the Last Dragon: A Life of Edwin Morgan *(2012: 178–80). At one point in their correspondence, Morgan rather disingenuously claims not to want to appear to be 'a cuckoo in the nest', and yet his objection to Redgrove's free approach continues from his warnings in the Hungarian broadcast, and indeed from his whole approach to translation as articulated from the 1950s onwards. Morgan was remorseless in his quest for accuracy, and Redgrove was unable or unwilling to produce the original rough translations by a Hungarian speaker on which his versions were based. The Hungarian academic and poet George Gömöri was contacted and endorsed Morgan's unease with them.*

The same critical eye was cast on 'Mountain Landscape' read in the broadcast. In Morgan's more accurate and idiomatic version, the concision of 'Nemo's song' and the monosyllabic final line clinches the vision:

MOUNTAIN LANDSCAPE
Valley brook
birdsong squabble.

High quiet
home of god-faced
rocks hanging.

And higher, Nemo's song,
hilltop, grindstone-squeal:
ice cracks smart.
(Transl. 6 May 1969. *CT*: 96)

A similar blending of natural syntax with mythopoeic or anthropological strangeness gives Morgan's 'Queen Tatavane' a different order of power:

QUEEN TATAVANE
O my winged ancestors!
Green branch and dry twig you gave me
for my two empires, to plant one and to lash one.
I am small as a weasel, pure as the eastern Moon,
light-ankled as a gazelle, but not poised for flight –
my heart is open to you, to every silent suggestion.

The Elephantstar took my fifteenth year,
the Dragonstar brought this, the sixteenth.
I am allowed three husbands by ancestral decree
and seven lovers beneath the holy jasmine leaves.

Not for me to escape with girl-friends to the fields,
for happy laughter, goats to milk, fresh milk to drink,
instead I sit on the throne in your light year after year,
an ebony idol with the world's weight on my neck.

Negro caravans, Arab ships are my traffic and merchandise,
I pay well, though I see most as polecats and monkeys,
but even the sky rains on unchosen ground, seeds burst unchosen.

I survey the naked hosts lost in their prison,
all of them I love as if they were my children,
punishing with the rod and if need be by the sword,
and though my heart should bleed my looks are frozen.
(Transl. May 1969. *CT*: 83–7)

*Preparing for publication with his usual thoroughness, Morgan contacted Weöres for details of the origins of mythical names he had already researched without success (*The Midnight Letterbox: Selected Correspondence 1950–2010: 236*). They were a blend of obscure anthropology and sheer imagination, it transpired. The rhetoric of 'Queen Tatavane' may echo across decades into the dramatic versions of* Gilgamesh *which Morgan undertook in the 1990s, finally published as* The Play of Gilgamesh *(Carcanet, 2006). Morgan's translations of Weöres, and his comments on Hungarian poetry, were extended in* Sandor Weöres: Eternal Moment. Selected Poems, *ed. Miklós Vajda (Corvina and Anvil Press, 1988) and in* The Colonnade of Teeth: Modern Hungarian Poetry, *eds George Gömöri and George Szirtes (Bloodaxe Books, 1996).*

Attila József's influence had an even greater time-span. Morgan first came across József's poetry in the early 1950s, in a small collection in Italian translation with facing Hungarian text. He found himself engaged not only by this urban poetry in Italian (in which he would have been fairly confident through his reading of Montale and the Renaissance poets) but also by the experience of looking across the page to see what the original language was like. So his first 'reading' of Hungarian poetry was as bi- or tri-lingual as modern Hungarian poets had needed to become through the exceptional nature of their language and history. When pressed by his interviewer Attila Dósa for Hungarian poems he had particularly enjoyed translating, Morgan mentions 'Night in the Suburbs':

I think especially because I was brought up in Glasgow in an environment that couldn't have been all that different from the Budapest of his time. [...] I had very strong feelings about Glasgow: what an industrial city was like, how people lived in it and so on. So when I saw József's city poems I liked them very much and wanted to make good translations of them. I like to see a very sharp, powerful poetry of life in the industrial city. Later, of course, I got into other aspects of his work, like his love poetry or his poems about his family. But the first thing that struck me about it was the idea of an industrial urban landscape, very often involving completely modern imagery: for instance the trains that are running through his poetry, of course with a final tragic outcome. [...] Well, I would qualify it by saying that although I found these tremendously interesting, the ones that probably moved me most were the ones about his mother [...]. The one just called 'Mother', an elegy on his mother and the washing she had to undertake to make a living. I think it is a very good poem. A wonderful poem! (*Beyond Identity*: 46)

As in his translations of Weöres, Morgan worked against contemporary practice that he felt had missed the form and spirit of József. Published in the same year as his trip to Budapest, Attila József: Poems, *edited by Thomas Kabdebo with translations by Michael Hamburger, Thomas Kabdebo, Vernon Watkins et al. (London: Danubia Book Company. 1966), provided some examples of what not to do. Here is 'Mother' as translated by Vernon Watkins, a not inconsiderable poet missing the mark:*

MOTHER
For a week now, again and again,
Thoughts of my mother have racked my brain.
Gripping a basket of washing fast,
On, and up to the attic she passed.
And I was frank and released my feeling
In stamps and yells to bring down the ceiling.
Let someone else have the bulging jackets,
Let her take me with her up to the attic.
She just, giving me no look or thrashing,
Went on, and in silence spread out the washing,
And the kneaded clothes, rustling brightly,
Were twisting and billowing up lightly.
I should not have cried but it's too late for this.
Now I can see what a giant she is.
Across the sky her grey hair flickers through;
In the sky's waters she is dissolving blue.

Michael Hamburger, as might be expected, does better with 'Night in the Suburbs', although neither his nor Morgan's versions is selected for The Colonnade of Teeth: Modern Hungarian Poetry, *with the honours going to the team of Lucas Myers and Agnes Vadas. (Morgan is the most frequently chosen translator for József, but Vernon Watkins also appears.):*

NIGHT ON THE OUTSKIRTS
Slowly the light's net is lifted
Out of the yard, and our kitchen
Fills with darkness
Like the hollows deep in a pool.
Silence –
The scrubbing brush creeps to life,
Above it, a patch of wall
Hesitates, hangs, not sure
Whether to stay or fall.
A night that wears oily rags
Heaves a sigh,
Halts in the sky;
Then settles on the outskirts,
Waddles over the square
And lights a bit of moon to see by.

Morgan would return to translating both József and Weöres in the 1980s and '90s, and it could be argued that his choice of these poets as guiding voices might have something to do with his own developing sense of Scottish identity. That argument is for another time, of course, but in revisiting the broadcast that emerged from his Hungarian notebook I was struck by his description of poetry as 'a great instrument of national identity', and of the history of Hungary under its invaders and oppressors from east and west as 'the dogged persistence of an entity, small, unique, islanded, self-aware'. Oppressors can come from different points of the compass, and Scotland is peninsula-ed rather than islanded. But the self-awareness of this small, unique tri-lingual country has been strangely enhanced by coming at it externally, as it were, through translation.

The work of translation is not without its occupational hazards. In NHQ XXVII: 102 Summer 1986, Morgan translated six poems by László Kálnoky, all uncollected except 'The Fatties at the Baths' (CT: 410–11). Selecting translations for the 'Collected', he found that much good work had to be omitted for practical reasons of space and cost. Possibly this was the case with 'The Translator's Death', composed by Kálnoky in 1953 and translated by Morgan in May 1986. It is a sad/funny piece of health and safety advice, later published by Gömöri and Szirtes in The Colonnade of Teeth. *But in electing not to collect this poem, Morgan may simply have been signalling that there was far too much still to be done before he could lay down his translator's pen. And indeed he kept translating through the 1990s and into the final post-millennial decade of his life.*

THE TRANSLATOR'S DEATH
Twenty years further on, what will I be like?
I think of it more and more, with less and less delight.
Hacked and battered, grey and bald, thin as a rake,
my study an espresso bar for old times' sake,
I'll sit there scribbling, to cup after cup
of caffeine euphoria, my artery walls
growing sclerotic and silting up
just to remind me of coffins and palls.
Yet it's not the embolism, the cerebral haemorrhage
that brings the threat. My end is more strange:
the lifelong translator must litter the stage
shot like the mark on a rifle-range.

When I die, I hope you will all laugh out loud,
don't let pity lie on your hearts like a cloud.
Pass your strictest judgements upon me:
'Well, at last this fool has got his fee,
he knew what he was after, pouring his life's blood
into a succession of alien spirits, proud
to meet a new commission for his pen
by slicing his heart like an onion-skin.
What if it was his sweet treasure, his talent, he chose
to sell it mercilessly, like glucose.
So he emptied himself bit by bit
till he was a bag of bones... which broke and split.
And now? He's ripe and ready for trash city.'
Don't hold me back with mercy, don't give me pity.

Beautiful Writing

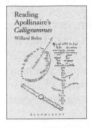

Willard Bohn, *Reading Apollinaire's* Calligrammes (Bloomsbury), £79.20

Reviewed by
BEVERLEY BIE BRAHIC

'Is Apollinaire France's greatest twentieth-century poet?' someone mused at a London literary event a few years ago. I hadn't thought of him in that light, because his early death, aged thirty-eight, in 1918, might seem to make him an unlikely candidate for a twentieth-century-spanning honour. Upon reflection, though, Apollinaire, né Guillaume-Albert-Wladimir-Alexandre-Apollinaire-Kostrowitsky (there are different spellings) in Rome on 26 August 1880 of an unknown father and a Polish mother, might well be my nominee – if I can discount the claims of some who have written on into the twenty-first century, and the cerebral Valéry. In *Calligrammes,* the subject of Professor Bohn's new book, Apollinaire shows himself to be an astonishingly vivid, wide-ranging and experimental poet. He was also an art critic and the author of some deliciously licentious tales.

To read Apollinaire alongside Rupert Brook and Wilfred Owen is to rub one's eyes in disbelief – imagine Vanessa Bell discovering Matisse. A fellow traveller of the young century's most subversive painters – Picasso, Braques, Sonia and Robert Delaunay, Matisse and the 'gentle' Rousseau, whose tombstone is engraved with an Apollinaire poem: 'Let our baggage pass free through heaven's gate / We'll bring you brushes, paints and canvases / So you can devote your sacred leisures / In the Real light to painting /... the Face of the stars' – Apollinaire was also a forerunner of the post-war Surrealists. Indeed, until 1914, when his enlistment in France's 38th Artillery Regiment made him a war poet, Apollinaire thought to call his new collection *Me Too, I'm a Painter.* This collection would have included *Calligrammes* – poems like 'Windows', a Cubist or 'Simultaneist' time-and-space-collapsing construction penned for the 1913 Delaunay exhibit catalogue. Here, to illustrate the poet's exuberance, are its last four lines (Apollinaire had dispensed with punctuation already in his also marvellous 1913 collection, *Alcools*):

From red to green all the yellow dies
Paris Vancouver Hyères Maintenon New York and the Antilles
The window opens like an orange
Lovely fruit of the light

'At first glance, "Les Fenêtres" resembles a shopping list more than a poem,' Professor Bohn comments. 'Each line consists of a single, isolated phrase, often lacking a verb, which is juxtaposed with two equally isolated phrases above and below. [...] There are no conjunctions or other grammatical devices to link various themes and motifs.' Apollinaire, especially pleased with this poem, confided to a friend: 'I have done my best to simplify poetic syntax, and at times I've succeeded, notably in one poem: "Windows".'

Calligrammes was influenced by the 1909 Futurist Manifesto in its celebration of speed, travel, progress, machines and, more controversially, violence (with characteristic lightness, and irony, Apollinaire calls battle flares 'glittery dancers', a trench 'the thunder's small palace' and compares artillery to 'champagne bottles... in which blood ferments'). But there is also melancholy pink- and-blue-period work featuring saltimbancos ('A Ghost of Clouds'), dear also to Baudelaire and Picasso; as well as the flattened, layered surfaces and semi-abstractions of the Cubists ('Windows', 'Lundi Rue Christine'), not forgetting the calligrammes ('beautiful writing') themselves: poems like ink drawings ('Rain', for instance, lettered in long, slanted lines). *Reading Apollinaire's* Calligrammes reproduces four of these (does this explain its price?); more can be viewed online.

We can only speculate what Apollinaire might have written had he survived the war and the 1918 flu pandemic. *Calligrammes'* last poems, 'Victory' and 'The Pretty Redhead' (also an epithalamion), are poetic manifestoes:

O mouths men are seeking a new language
Which no grammarian of any language will find fault with
And these old languages are so close to death
Truly it's out of habit and for lack of daring
That we still use them for poetry

[...] But let's keep trying to talk
Flap our tongues
Splutter and spit
Let's have new sounds new sounds new sounds...

~

We want to offer you some vast and strange domains
Where mystery holds out its flower to whoever would pick it
There are new fires colours never before seen
A thousand imponderable fantasies
To be made real

– lines that have influenced several generations of avant-garde American poets beginning with the New York School's francophile John Ashbery and Kenneth Koch, who also worked eagerly with painters.

Professor Bohn offers close readings of nineteen poems, in seven thematic and largely chronological chapters. Each poem is contextualised biographically and literarily, paraphrased and interpreted, in part through a rather clumsily integrated compilation of the comments of other scholars ('Writing in 1971, Norma Rinsler noted... As Els Jongeneel recently complained... as Michel Décaudin declares... as Décaudin and Lockerbie point out' pp. 123–4). Sometimes these comments seem too obvious to warrant citation: 'Throughout the war poetry, Greet and Lockerbie note, stars are constantly compared to shells and vice versa.' Still, if *Reading Apollinaire's* Calligrammes introduces Apollinaire's exciting, and readable poems to new readers, one must rejoice.

Cock-crow

Richard Scott, *Solo* (Faber), £10.99

Reviewed by GREGORY WOODS

Richard Scott opens a library copy of *The Golden Treasury* and, to compensate for its lack of gay poems, writes 'COCK' in the margin. In an act of queering that prefigures the writer he will later become, he doodles obscenities and adds a few choice quotations of his own, to supplement what must have seemed a pretty tinny treasury. I say Richard Scott does this, but it may only be the speaker of his poem 'Public Library, 1998', the first in this collection, who does. At any rate, it is Scott who writes 'COCK' in the margin of the poem.

There is more than whiff of the library about *Soho*. In his up-front Acknowledgements page, Scott goes the whole Kate Winslet, thanking not only the usual magazines, funders, editors and loved ones, but also Shakespeare, Socrates, Rilke, Hopkins, Genet, Eliot, Freud; and a whole swag of queer theorists: Valerie Traub, Eve Sedgwick, David Halperin, Leo Bersani, Michel Foucault...

In an interview on the Forward Arts Foundation website, Scott calls this 'an openly queer book, which is about gay shame, the search for homosexual ancestry and the vulnerability of queer bodies'. This sets it outside the boundaries of the the rainbow-flaggy, commercial version of gayness. 'I am the homosexual you / cannot be proud of', he says in one poem. No doubt uncomfortably for some readers, he is engaged in a serious task of putting the shame back into shameless. (One of the epigraphs dotted through the book is from Sedgwick: 'Shame, too, makes identity'.) His is a library right in the heart of things, narrowly personal and broadly political.

The opening section, 'Admission' (with an epigraph from Whitman), admits the reader into what the writer admits, whether on his own account or his speakers'. It starts with a poem ('crocodile') about being raped as a child. 'Fishmonger' is about being abused in the back of a van. Scott is getting used to being asked if these poems refer to experiences of his own: 'is the I you'. In a poem itself called 'Admission':

> he asks if my poems are authentic
> do I have any experience in the matter
> and by this he means abuse
> and by this he means have I been a victim

Later in the predictable conversation, 'he cites Wordsworth something familiar / about tranquillity'. That there ever is tranquillity in which to be reflective about rape is a big assumption. If there is 'admission' or confession here, it is reined in by this qualifying argument about authenticity. When Scott begins a poem 'are you looking for me in these lines' the tone sounds like Whitman's ('This is no book; / Who touches this, touches a man'), but the anxiety not.

As for 'homosexual ancestry', this is not a mere matter of naming influences. The search is for mentors and exemplars, as man-loving male poets, but also, more generally, as queer bodies and tongues. To take just the example of Whitman, he is constantly being befriended and re-voiced by gay poets – Carpenter, Crane, Lorca, Pessoa, Ginsberg – who pay homage to him, not to claim some ossified cultural tradition of homo-eroticism (as so many homosexual men had affirmed a conservative allegiance to the Greeks and their statuesque ephebes), but in search of a method and a language with which, in close reference to the details of modern life, to say the unsayable, while doing it, too.

Soho's second section has gorgeous demolitions and re-molitions of Verlaine. These ravaged versions are less translations than a parasitic invasion, feeding on the crude essence of Verlaine from within and bursting out with a recrudescence both perfumed and mephitic. Here and in his versions of Vincenzo Bellini's arias, he winkles out and develops the perversities we've grown used to ignoring in high culture's stilted politeness.

Scott counters bland LGBT pieties ('*it gets better*') with sacrileges of his own ('*there'll always be haters* / only you'll be older'). Even in an age of equal marriage and why-label-yourself, we carry the wounds of homophobia. We know from the history of AIDS that the crumbs of acceptance can be grabbed back without notice. We know that, even if we ourselves are safe, others are not:

> When I read how they poured petrol over that man
> I see my own death in some outlying federal province.

Scott's reading, theory included, is connected to sensors of pleasure and pain, both personal and collective. The erotic poems are never merely about bodies. Encounters are arranged and poems drafted on smartphones (hence, no doubt, the lower-case habit). Love is prostheticised with plugs and apps, books and mags, nail bombs and Local Government Acts, semen and bleach. Perhaps the best we can hope for is to be 'free from shame but made from shame'. I think of the Orphic body, singing on while piecing itself together again; recovery mode.

Distancing himself from himself even while maintaining the strictest of auto-intimacies, Richard Scott writes a poem 'in the style of richard scott' ('in the style of': another borrowing from Verlaine) in which 'it hurts everyday so I read'. He lists some favourite queer writers by their first names. Comforting, perhaps, but this is only 'in the style of', as if his own were just one of many styles to use as formative exercises. This seems an inversion or invagination of 'Thom': even *out of* bed I pose.

Soho 'crescendos to' (as its flyleaf unfortunately puts it) the long closing poem, 'O my Soho!', which dances through gay history in a manner as hectic as it is haphazard. Among other things, it revisits the old debate between polite assimilation and a rigorously maintained queerness. It uses the British Museum's frothily charged Warren Cup as an example of how things work: it is a 'Uranian chalice of Victorian naivety', respectably valued for its access to the ancient sources of civilisation. Should we be grateful for this? Tasteful touring exhibitions of the buffed-up Cup? Cue Peggy Lee: is *that* all there is?

Anyway, it's good to see this intelligent and rather harrowingly beautiful book in the Faber livery, snooking a cock at T.S. ('awful daring of a moment's surrender') Eliot.

The General Chaos of the World

Maximianus, *The Elegies*, edited and translated by A. M. Juster, with an introduction by Michael Roberts (University of Pennsylvania Press), $65

Reviewed by EVAN JONES

In the Western imagination, whenever anyone talks of the glory and splendour of Rome, this really means the Empire's first three hundred years. These held a position of glamour and intrigue through the last century (think *I, Claudius*, *Memoirs of Hadrian*, *Doctor Who and the Romans*). That there was equally a quieter interest in the empire's Republican days or its slow tectonic movement east tells as much about where modernists and postmodernists saw themselves as it does about the way in which the West viewed itself. The ideals of the imperial held sway, even as world wars were fought for the sake of democracy. Into the twenty-first century, and the era of the Late Empire and what is called Byzantium (but whose people referred to themselves as Romans) has started to return to favour. This is, in one sense, Gibbon's decline. But in another, and it's preferable, this is the origins of what happened next: the Renaissance.

The elegies of the late-Roman poet Maximianus (c. sixth century AD) are quiet and plain-spoken. He appears to have lived in the era of the Western reconquests of the Christian Emperor Justinian, flavourfully retold in Robert Graves's less-famous *Count Belisarius* (1938). He may be the same Maximianus sent to the court of Justinian, detailed in the fifth elegy, about whom a letter is extant (translated and included in an appendix here). Yet the Maximianus of the elegies was a pagan, an inheritor of Horace, Juvenal and Ausonius, set apart from the Christian verse of the era (his near-contemporary, Romanus Melodus, for example). And the popularity of his elegies was such that they served for centuries as a teaching tool. Chaucer knew the elegist well enough that translated lines appear in *The Canterbury Tales*. And W. H. Auden, in an unpublished essay commissioned for *Life* magazine in 1966, wrote of Maximianus:

> How much more moving to us than Virgil's description of the military triumphs depicted on Aeneas' shield is the following incident in one of Maximian's elegies. Sent by Theodoric as an envoy to Constantinople, he picks up a girl. He is getting on in years and proves impotent. The girl starts to cry. He tries to comfort her by assuring her that she can easily find a more adequate lover. 'It's not that', she says, 'it's the general chaos of the world'.

A.M. Juster, pen name of Michael James Astrue, a lawyer and former commissioner of the Social Security Administration under Presidents Bush and Obama, translates the scene, moving from the Latin distich into 'couplets in alternating iambic hexameter and iambic pentameter', like this:

> 'Woman, while you lament the slackness of my prick,
>   you show you suffer from a worse disease.'

> She raged, 'You're clueless, traitor! Clueless, as I see it!
>   I mourn a public, not a private, hell...

This, the end of the fifth elegy, continues for forty-four lines, in the girl's voice – what Michael Roberts in his introduction calls, a 'hymn to the penis'. Sort of. On the one hand the baser reading is, okay, sure. But on the other, what Auden describes is tender and heartfelt, the movement from private to public worries, the girl lamenting that the dysfunction of the male member is symptomatic. The metaphor of Maximianus's impotence becomes a poetic failure.

And behind the metaphor of aging, Maximianus's chief theme is failure. The six elegies list the difficulties of growing old, lists and lists, offering no solutions, only a sort of stoic long-suffering through the betrayals of body and the betrayals of love. Once he won prizes and acclaim, love and sexual conquest, now he doesn't, poor man. That these early achievements might not hold the value he attributes to them isn't an issue.

Elements of Maximianus's back-and-forth quotidian misery are similar to Sir Francis Bacon's 'The Life of Man', the give and take of the pains of life, but Maximianus is more focused:

> It's better being full; soon being full annoys.
>   It's best I fast; it's painful to have fasted.

> With food that served well once, the opposite returns;
>   repelled, one throws away what once was sweet.

This is what Maximianus offers us: through a reading of a man's old age, an understanding of the limitations of his ambition and desire. But more, in the fifth elegy, the larger cost of those limitations. The girl recognises that 'these schemes that are opposed to Venus', in her sixth-century world, bloody, violent, wars and politicians, lions and lambs – all lay down before male pleasure. She argues: What's to become of a man, undermined by agedness? And what's to become of her, little more than an object of desire in that man's world? She may be the most sympathetic woman in all of Latin literature. She isn't given a name.

The language of Juster's translation can seem overly formal and even stuffily nineteenth-century ('Alas, they witness something grim and frenzied!'). But he is a skilled reader of Latin and his commentary elucidates a text that has been unavailable in a scholarly English translation for too long. Maximianus is relevant again in his irrelevance: his elegies capture the pain and futility of life, the need to make something in this existence, which can only result in slow, inevitable failure. The fifth elegy ends: 'At last she shuts up, satisfied by boundless grief. / She leaves me as if my last rites were over.'

Love shook my heart

Philip Freeman, *Searching for Sappho: The Lost Songs and World of the First Woman Poet* (Norton), $15.95

Reviewed by SUE LEIGH

There have been many books by scholars for scholars on Sappho but American academic Philip Freeman describes his *Searching for Sappho* as 'a book for everyone else'. And it is just that. Some parts – for example, Grenfell and Hunt's discovery in Egypt in 1897 of papyrus with lines by Sappho – read like a detective story. Other passages bring the ancient world vividly alive with well-chosen detail. The book also includes Freeman's own translations of all the surviving poems and fragments, including those most recently discovered.

Freeman sets out to explore the life, poetry and world of Sappho. Biographical facts he admits are few and some questionable. We do know she was born on Lesbos in the seventh century BCE into a wealthy merchant family, that she had three brothers and her mother was Cleis. We cannot be certain, however, who her father was or the name of her husband (the latter might have been Cercylas according to the *Suda*, a tenth-century encyclopaedia). She did have a much loved daughter also named Cleis. Sappho was exiled in Sicily around 600 BCE and presumably returned to Lesbos, where she died in old age.

The book's concern, however, is to get a sense of Sappho's life from her poetry. That is challenging as much of it has survived only as fragments. Some come from ancient papyri, pottery shards and mummy wrappings found in Egypt. But more than half of the two hundred or so more substantial poems and fragments are to be found as quotations in the works of ancient male writers such as the 'Ode to Aphrodite' (the only complete poem) embedded in a book on literary composition by the critic Dionysius of Halicarnassus. Freeman reminds us that discoveries continue – as recently as 2014 two more poems were found, 'The brothers' and a short poem about unrequited love.

Sappho's poetry was largely lyric poetry and would have been sung to the accompaniment of a lyre. The poems are unusual for their time in their use of the lyric 'I' and also the poet's voice which is intimate, personal. They are frequently addressed to women or friends. Their subject matter often relates to loss, nature, love, desire. 'Love shook my heart / like a mountain wind falling on oaks', she writes.

Freeman sees Sappho's poetry as a woman's voice speaking out in an age dominated by men. The poems, he writes, 'give us a window into the lives of all women in ancient Greece' and help us understand the different stages in a woman's life. What was it like to be a young girl over two thousand years ago? What was the experience of marriage and motherhood like for the majority of women? How did a woman's life change as she grew older? He uses this framework to structure the book so there are chapters on childhood, marriage, sexuality, religion and death (with fascinating details of social customs, medicinal knowledge, religious rites and so on). Each of the chapters is illustrated with extracts from the poems of Sappho and the work of other classical poets such as Catullus, Ovid, Erinna, Alcman.

Freeman's translations of the poems are fresh and contemporary, though for me they don't have the precision of Anne Carson's *If Not, Winter: Fragments of Sappho* (Carson tries to translate nothing which is not in the Greek, and to follow the original word order and line breaks as far as possible). Freeman, like Carson, loves the spaces between words in the fragments – what Carson calls the 'free space of imaginal adventure'.

This is a fascinating guide to the world of Sappho: well researched, lively and accessible. The book should give readers new to her work an excellent introduction; and those more familiar with it, new insights into the work of the poet Plato called the tenth muse.

Having Ears

Angela Leighton, *Hearing Things: The Work of Sound in Literature* (Belknap Press), £25.95

Reviewed by RICHARD PRICE

This is a book primarily about the theme of listening in Anglophone poetry. Virginia Woolf, Alice Munro, and (very briefly) Toni Morrison, extend it beyond verse: the author argues for a lyric sensibility in fiction which surely all three of these writers share, a case particularly well made in Leighton's treatment of Woolf, Tennyson and *To The Lighthouse*.

Questions Leighton asks include: How can birdsong in generations of verse mark key differences in sensibility as well as continuities of tradition? What might it mean to listen to a house? Why are horses heard through centuries of poetry? In what ways do poets who love and hate each other make inscribed acts of listening part of their strange exchange?

There are also intriguing questions raised about poetry as a listening and communicating device itself: well beyond poetry's ability to impart recently gleaned information, Leighton asks if poetry's peculiar ways of expressing things might themselves constitute a form of knowledge. She is tentative in asking this question, and tentative in answering it, almost as if the nature of the enquiry is actually at cross-purposes with the nature of poetry. As Leighton notes, Derek Attridge has suggested that poetry can be a way of performing knowledge – as music is – but cannot easily be a way of knowing itself, unless the terms of knowing have to be revised beyond the emphasis on imparting information which 'knowledge' tends to carry by convention. Perhaps an animal kind of knowledge is what this is about. If learning to love watching people dancing and hearing people singing, so that the body resonates with movement and melody whether or not we become dancers or singers ourselves, is knowledge, then perhaps there is an equivalent and related resonance – we ourselves dance, we hum a tune, we 'poetry' (a new verb). This may be 'informationless' but still a profound form of knowledge. Maybe it isn't knowledge, but it is deep.

Leighton is especially interested in the self-listening act of silent reading, and this makes me think of the Celtic Roman St Ambrose, who lived in the fourth century. He was perhaps the first person documented as a silent reader, as recounted by another of the early 'fathers' of the church, the African Roman Augustine. This was clearly unusual practice. Augustine perversely suggests this made Ambrose much more interruptible than 'normal' readers who read aloud. I can just imagine Ambrose cursing – silently of course – those who misinterpreted his preference for quiet contemplation as licence to strike up a conversation with him at any time.

Today, a line of mockery is to suggest that someone's lips move as they read, but in Augustine's day it looks as if something, if not opposite, certainly very different, was at play: to fully sound out the words as one read was to be in a formal relationship with language and a public, and so it would be quite a serious act to interrupt another reading aloud. In contrast, silent reading was not so self-protecting a practice as it would be thought of today; rather it was merely something 'private', and privacy would presumably come lower down in the moral hierarchy of a religious power than the public duty of being available to speak a text.

I don't imagine Ambrose was the first person to read silently, but its mention may mean it was a novelty at this point. Tellingly, Ambrose was otherwise renowned for very unquiet activities: he was a master of rhetoric as well as a figure in Milan's public life who others literally and dramatically *spoke up* for, vocal support leading to his becoming Bishop of Milan and later head of the Western Church. He is even known as championing antiphony's adoption in the church. It's therefore safe to say that when Ambrose read to himself he, of all people, was hypersensitive to the vocality of such interior reading.

In this way, Ambrose's silent reading should be seen as at the heart of the enigma which Angela Leighton's *Hearing Things* begins to address: the soundless performance of sound in silent reading, and, especially, the active listening such performance entails. Is it also not the case that certain kinds of silent reading do not involve this kind of internal sonic performance? – some texts are read too quickly for that and some take on a quality which is more visual or even more mathematical, so that their performance does not come to the fore. Most poetry would be of the 'silently sounded' kind, it is true, but perhaps not all.

As you can tell, I am pretty interested in these questions so felt tantalised by the author's raising of them at the beginning of the book, only to drop them until the concluding chapter. While this is a joyful, clever book, with no pretensions to comprehensiveness, there is a slightly miscellaneous feel to it, and some of the explicit de-scoping does rather raise an eyebrow. In Leighton's own words: no 'drama and performance poetry', very little literature from 'the heritage of black writing' whose 'logical end is the live audience rather than the solitary reader', and no work of singer-songwriters. Even more peculiar is the lack of engagement with, or even reference to, sound poetry itself, with Marinetti and Schwitters making no appearance. The only sound poet who does pop up, Edith Sitwell, does so in passing, in relation to Yeats and abstraction (Cocteau's *Orpheus* – surely dramatic poetry of a kind – also features, via Yeats and centaurs who tap out a non-vocal poetry with their hooves).

I think these absences are losses: such an approach fillets live performability, which surely conditions internal listening, from the private performance of the imagination. This perhaps is why despite the warning of known exclusions, the author then does use theatre, radio, known private readings, and song, albeit to evidence influence on printed texts, while steering clear of their deeper exposition.

[In the field I know best, songs, I think immediately of two great listening songs which would have added to Leighton's case. Tom Waits's dramatic monologue 'What's He Building in There?' performs a paranoid act of anti-neighbourliness, in part by compiling rumour with the aural texture of any household to build a portrait not of a dangerous neighbour but of a malign prejudiced listener. Leighton's fruitful analysis of the nursery rhyme 'Sing a Song of Sixpence' in Yeats, explored so interestingly by Leighton, all the same cries out (to me) for the inclusion of its later incarnation in The Beatles's 'Cry, Baby, Cry', where the royal fantasy of the traditional rhyme has morphed into an unsettling yet melancholy bourgeois mis-en-scene: the blackbirds of the old song are entirely absent, replaced by séance voices 'put on by the children for a lark' (there is a genius hint of vestigial 'birdyness' in that use of that word 'lark'). Even in terms of separating inert 'page poetry' from the live, a separation I would contend and complicate, those two lyrics, with their music absent, stand as fine page-wise as many a 'page lyric' in *Hearing Things,* and there are plenty more where they came from.]

Rightly rating Walter de la Mare, Leighton bends her own rules, persuading the reader of his significance on the basis of, among other things, the remarkable phenomenon of the live performance of his poetry – his work is still frequently requested on radio, and when Thomas Hardy was on his deathbed he didn't ask for a copy of de la Mare's 'The Listeners' to read to himself, he asked for someone to read it to him. Maybe the 'logical end' of de la Mare's work is, after all, a live audience. I would generalise this out to take in recent debates: is page poetry really primarily for a silent reader? I wonder.

In any case, Leighton is quite brilliant in tracing lineages of echo and influence between poets, figured particularly on sound (echoes of echoes). In this way, Christina Rossetti's debt to Tennyson, and yet her resolute differences, are convincingly portrayed; the murmuring of bees is followed delightfully from Tennyson to Yeats to Woolf and even, with a light touch, to Pooh Bear. De la Mare is rightly re-found in the company of Hardy, Frost and Thomas as significant peer, and there are productive readings of W. S. Graham, Jorie Graham and others. Alice Oswald, like de la Mare, is another curious anomaly in Leighton's own framing of the book, since Oswald is well-known and perhaps best known as a live performer, who reads her work from memory and at length – but in any case benefits from Leighton's focus on her eclipsed earlier poems. I also liked the wry self-portrait vignettes Leighton uses at the opening of chapters, too, including, an affectionate tribute to Shakespeare's non-appearing and so absolutely silent character, Moth.

Still Life

Matthew Sweeney, *My Life as a Painter*
(Bloodaxe), £9.95

Reviewed by RACHEL MANN

Even in these late times, there are certain proprieties around death. If it is possible (perhaps even *de rigueur*) to have a 'no-fuss direct cremation' funeral, one is not supposed to speak ill of the dead. *De Mortuis,* and all that. It may be superstition, inherited from our Roman forebears, but I've been alert to it as I've prepared to review Matthew Sweeney's twelfth volume of poetry. As I write, Sweeney has newly joined the great majority and I am alert to the challenge of writing critically about the work of one so freshly deceased. If all critics have long since imbibed the distinction between 'writer' and 'writing', recent death does tend to weigh on the mind. (My anxieties, I suspect, would amuse Sweeney greatly; if he could, he might even incorporate it into one of his characteristic pieces of surrealistic fancy.)

Tempting though it is, then, to see *My Life as a Painter* as a kind of culmination, I shall (mostly) resist. Sweeney writes, in the title poem, 'I often find a wish going through me to remake myself/as a painter.' It's a response to those lines of Frank O'Hara, offered as the collection's epigraph: 'I am not a painter. I am a poet. / Why? I think I would rather be / A painter, but I am not.' Sweeney's poem offers not so much a desire for a late change of vocation, as a reiteration of a familiar Sweeney trope: a way to play amusingly and surreally with a problem, a gambit (in this case, the story of a gun-toting father who kills birds for supper). If the poem is a meditation on death, it indicates an old point: morbidity finds a pleasing consistency when properly arranged. If he were a painter, Sweeney says, 'I'd stay faithful / to the old concept of the still life or, in French, *nature morte.*'

If Sweeney mostly resists the ekphrastic (Lowry makes a passing intervention as interlocutor), the visual returns again and again. 'The Man with the Pillow' explores the cinematic, in which Sweeney imagines himself as a cine-camera enthusiast who turns his subject into a construction of techniques: 'I'd focus on his face, his eyes / for a long time, like Orson Wells. I'd have Baltic jazz playing.' Sweeney's use of that old poetic trick, the subjunctive mood, is perfectly suited to his flights of fancy. In 'Google Maps', he claims, 'I feel I've nearly visited the moon, as I / chatted with a man who's been there. / And if I wanted to retrace his steps / Google Maps would lead me / unerringly to the Sea of Tranquility / or to the nightclubs of the dark side.'

Sweeney's oeuvre is imaginative play and *Life as a Painter* doesn't disappoint. Here is a cast of seagulls, rats and camels, a menagerie of the domestic and feral made subject to wit and close attention. It's something of a cliché to read gulls as the animal world's selfish bastards (a Disney film made great play of it fifteen years ago), but Sweeney's claim, 'The seagulls in Guernsey had been the Nazis / who'd conquered the island in the 40s', is great fun. In 'The Dance of the Rats' there is a more substantial desire to escape the confines of a human body. He says, 'I knew I'd scare them away, / so I contented myself with / imagining each with another's/tail in its mouth, and still / squeaks escaping them, making/a music that pleased me hugely.'

Some might take these flights as all sound and fury, though I'm not sure there would be any great sin in that. In 'Double Dirge', Sweeney writes, 'The owl rose above the dead dog / and hooted a five-blast night bird dirge / but the only creature that heard it / was the wasp that had stung the dog/and would expire before the morning.' Nothing lasts for long, and in Sweeney's world, the owl is immediately killed by a deaf boy with a fondness for playing dirges. If poetry is a kind of song, a dirge even, for Sweeney the fact that it be sung or played at all seems enough.

Perhaps, what is strongest in this final collection, is Sweeney's honesty, wrought not so much through poetic piety, but playfulness and disciplined strangeness. I want to resist treating *My Life as a Painter* as a culmination, but the closing poem, 'The Yellow Pole', rather breaks my resistance. Sweeney says, 'Paint the pole yellow,/stick it in the grave / of a poet, but make sure / the poet's lying there.' This pole is a totem; indeed, Sweeney speaks of 'the flag / of poetry, or of existence'. Sweeney suggests, 'Have a youthful friend / film it on her iPhone / ... while a toast to the poet / goes viral'. Finally, the pole is removed and launched into 'the swollen river.'

It is an adieu and a striking one. Rivers, of course, wash away, they cleanse and they carry their cargo to new destinations. They are – if one is of dramatic, Nordic bent – the means to carry away the final remains of the dead. Sweeney was no confessional poet, and all the better for that; he does not write his illness (Motor Neuron Disease) in these poems. Rather, ultimately, he is interested in language's capacity for alchemy; his transformations are made in surreal wit. It's not a bad farewell.

Feelinks

Sophie Herxheimer, *Velkom to Inklandt. Poems in My Grandmother's Inklisch* (Short Books), £12.99

Reviewed by DAVID C. WARD

The modern rule for writing in dialect – i.e. rendering spelling as if the words were spoken, usually by a subordinate, marginal or excluded ethnic group – is that you have to be a member of the group in order to do it. This may go without saying these days, when we like to think we've made progress on issues of race but for a long time it was not the norm in literature. The temptation to render the sonic qualities of the 'colourful' speech of African Americans, Cockneys and Jews (to name only three) has frequently proven irresistible, raising difficult questions about language, literature and hierarchy. The sibilant 'Sssss' with which Jewish characters announce themselves makes for uncomfortable reading. In the United States, a long 'tradition' of whites speaking as blacks now makes for uncomfortable reading however well-intentioned the author was. Or is: just this week a poem published in *The Nation* by a white writer came under fire and was disavowed by the journal's editors for using street slang and African American diction to express the point of view of a handicapped street person. The red flag of cultural appropriation was raised and the poem immediately became something other than a poem. Questions of race and exclusion aside, there is also just something stylistically odd about books that use standard English, the norm and hence colourless, and then launch into dialect when an Irishman or an African American appears.

From the inside, using vernacular language is both a sign of group identity and a vantage point from which both to assess one's exclusion and to critique the dominant culture even to the point of offering a proto-nationalist alternative. Political issues are always implicit in the use of language even when deployed in such an affectionate and charming way as Sophie Herxheimer does in her *Velkom to Inklandt*, her poems in her maternal grandmother's Leisel's voice. Leisel, her scientist husband and family emigrated from Berlin to London in 1938 and, at least according to Herxheimer, her English was always heavily accented. The opening poem 'London', when the bus conductor says 'Fanks Luv!': 'Zit is ven I know zat here to settle iss OK. Zis / City vill ve Home, ver effen on ze Buss is Luff.' It's worth noting that Leisel knew English apparently before she emigrated since there are no poems about her struggling to understand the language. Understanding the culture was something else again and the majority of the book is about Leisel's half comic, half exasperated attempts to come to terms with both wider society as well as her own family. The voice is realistic, practical and brisk. She sums up her 'Merritch':

> Ve velue ze Intellect apuff ze Tittel-Tettel.
> He likes to vurk, oont go to bett viz uzzer Vimmin.
> I like ze Parks, to voork, oont do ze Garten.
> Ze Children read, do Zums, pass zair Exems.

The conclusion: 'Who are ve? Ve are chest normall Peepl. / Two off ze Pork eating Choos off olt Inklant.' As with the infidelity, being Jewish is not much remarked on because Leisel takes it for granted, being only amused when 'ze Vooman' next door 'kryse / out in metd Inraichment: / *Go avay – you blutty Forennas!*' Leisel could teach the English stoicism. The tone is always to just get on, live your life, and don't let feelings in where they might do harm: 'Feelinks are romentik Rubbisch. / Somesink zat ze yunker Peepl hef –' When once she lets the feelings out – meeting a man at an art exhibition – she quickly stifles the instinct and gets on with the life she has accepted. Be resilient, the book ends, 'Chainch ideas ve must: or Dedt ve stay!'

It takes a little while to get into the rhythm and meaning of these poems but it's the dialect that gives them meaning as poems; if you 'translate' them into plain English they disappear because it's the charm of Leisel's distinctive voice that draws us in. Which raises a final question: Is this Leisel speaking or Sophie Herxhemier? The latter, of course. Leisel is visible only through the screen of language constructed by her granddaughter. One wonders if Leisel, inhabiting the cosmopolitan and intellectual world of the mid-century Jewish intelligentsia, would have appreciated being rendered in dialect. The question of assimilation – what you keep and what you discard as an émigré – is a difficult one and language is always contested terrain. Was Leisel quite as domestic as these poems suggest? The no nonsense dismissal of 'feelinks' can't be taken as given. Her voice is so singular that one would like to know a bit more about what this vigorous and shrewd woman thought about the wider world outside her family life. In her generous homage to her grandmother, has Sophie Herxheimer trapped her in her own rendition of her speech? That's the problem with identity politics: whose identity? whose politics?

The Inescapable Past

Robin Robertson, *The Long Take*
(Picador), £14.99

Reviewed by JOHN CHALLIS

In a departure from the folkloric concerns of his recent collections *The Wrecking Light* and *Hill of Doors*, Robin Robertson's new book-length, novelistic poem takes the underside of post-World War II America as its subject. Influenced by film noir, a style of cinema often characterised by its heavy use of chiaroscuro and its pessimistic, anxious tone, *The Long Take* critiques America's booming cities through the eyes of Walker, a traumatised D-Day veteran, who goes to LA to escape his past and gradually comes to consider how 'cities are a kind of war'.

Written in both prose and verse, the poem is fluid and formally loose. Robertson's attempts to create poetic versions of a range of filmic devices such as jump cuts, flashbacks and dream sequences, lend a distinctively cinematic structure to the narrative. Particularly effective is his ability to generate a physical dimension to the sense of claustrophobia and anxiety felt by Walker:

> The city's gone.
> In its place, this gray stone maze, this
> locked geometry of shadows, blind and black,
> and angles hurt into the sky, symmetries breaking
> and snapping back into line.
> The green Zs of fire-escapes; wires criss-
> crossing what's left of the light
> to a tight mesh.
> The buildings close
> around a dead-end, then
> spring open to the new future: repetition,
> back-tracking, error, loss.

Elsewhere, flashbacks triggered by the urban environment cut cinematically to Walker's memories of war. In these we are reminded of Robertson's gift for describing the gruesome with horrific and visual clarity: 'Right next to me, young Benjamin took some shrapnel in the throat: his windpipe torn open, so he's gargling blood and staring at me, fumbling at his neck like he feels his napkin is slipping.' When juxtaposed with a commentary on LA's obsessive rebuilding, the city and warzone begin to converge to create a particularly disorientating effect, cutting between the past and present to provide an analogy for Walker's experience. The above quote is immediately followed by: 'The scrape and whine of metal on stone. The drumfire of falling buildings.'

Gradually it becomes clear that Robertson is using film noir and its hard-boiled antecedents not for the purposes of pastiche, but to apply its anxious and shadowy texture to his chronicling of the changing topography of LA. His engagement with environmental change, social cleansing and homelessness in this cinematic and warlike version of LA posits *The Long Take* as an engrossing study of the development of a megalopolis and the corruption involved in building it, which resonates with similar contemporary anxieties.

Aside from attempts at creating a cinematic style, *The Long Take* does not wear its influence lightly. In over two hundred pages it references over twenty classic films noir: Walker crosses paths with film noir directors such as Robert Siodmak and Joseph H. Lewis, and inadvertently finds himself on the set of several films. References like these not only lend the poem cultural context, but demonstrate how Robertson makes use of both the creative representations of post-war anxiety in America alongside its historical causes (the threat of communism, the bomb) to provide several readings of the city. On one hand the city is a cinematic construct suspended by silver screen nostalgia, and on the other it is obsessed with demolition and renewal with a cannibalistic and warlike fervour. As Walker laments: 'American cites have no past, no history. Sometimes I think the only American history is on film.' It's fitting then that Walker finds solace in a place where the past is endlessly reimagined for the screen.

Exit Wounds

Carl Phillips, *Wild Is the Wind* (Farrar, Straus and Giroux), $23

Reviewed by FLORIAN GARGAILLO

> I know death's
> an abstraction, but I prefer
> a shape to things, though the shapes
> are changeable.
>   ('If You Go Away')

These lines tell us much about the sort of poetry to be found here, in Carl Phillips' fourteenth collection. His aim throughout is to take subjects of a metaphysical nature and shape them into sound, image and rhetoric.

It comes as little surprise, then, that abstractions populate the book and serve as its chief players. In order of appearance: *memory, discipline, morality, honesty, regret, indifference, death, power, history, love, trust, hope, despair,* and so on. Sometimes Phillips dresses these up in startling metaphors, as when he dismisses – and thereby evokes – the notion of memory as a 'mechanical bull' ('Wild Is the Wind').

This approach makes the abstractions livelier than they might be, though as agents they remain oddly passive:

> – So here we are again, one-handedly fingering
>   the puckered edges of the exit wounds
>   memory leaves behind
>   ('Givingly')

Memory here cuts flesh, and shapes that wound by giving it 'puckered edges' like lips readied for a kiss. Yet the word 'memory' itself gets shuttled all the way down to the third line so that it lands as an afterthought. The verb attached to it is not 'wounds', which stands as its own noun, but 'leaves behind': a letting-go or a giving-up. Abstractions in this volume are wont to become places: 'Morality seemed an ignorable wilderness / like any other...' ('Musculature'). And, more hazily, spaces: 'When did honesty become so hard to step into and stay / inside of...' ('Musculature').

Phillips is a writer who would always hover at the edge of meaning. That sensibility makes the poems by turns richly ambiguous and queasily evasive. The syntax has a habit of retreating into the obscurity of *its* and *theys* and *things*:

> Not knowing exactly what it's / come to is so much differ-
> ent from understanding that it's come
> to nothing. Why is it, then, each day, they feel more the same?
> ('Brothers in Arms')

> Sometimes
> we want a thing more than we can admit we
> want that thing.
> ('The Distance and the Spoils')

> There's a light that can make
> finding a thing look more than faintly
> like falling across it – you must kneel,
> make an offering.
> ('That It Might Save, or Drown Them')

Many of the poems end by disappearing into clouds of sentiment:

> Rest. Lean against me.
> ('The Distance and the Spoils')

> All my life, I've stowed what I loved most
> safe away.
> ('Black and Copper in a Crush of Flowers')

And then there is the vagueness that haunts so many of the book's images. 'His Master's Voice' gives us some 'indistinguishable brown birds' doing 'their dust-bath thing', while the flocks in 'Rockabye' 'fly like the storm-shook shadows / of themselves, and not like birds'. For Phillips, the things of the world exist primarily as metaphors through which his meditations can be made tangible, so that one wishes for a little more world and a little less mind.

These habits are hardly new, but in previous books Phillips had been more willing to play around with his abstractions. 'Youth with Satyr, Both Resting', from *Cortège* (1995), is one example of that earlier attitude:

> There are certain words – *ecstasy, abandon,*
> *surrender* – we can wait all our lives,
> sometimes,
>
> not so much to sue
> as to use correctly:
> then the moment at last comes,
>
> the right scene but more impossibly
> different than any we'd earlier imagined
> and we stumble, catching
>
> instead at nouns like *desire*, that
> could as easily be verbs,
> unstable adjectives like *rapt* or *unseemly*.

In *Wild Is the Wind*, however, Phillips leans on the atmosphere generated by words like 'desire' or 'ecstasy', rarely probing their implications or expanding on their possibilities. The best poems are the ones where his reluctance to pin anything down yields powerful nuances:

> For the gods in Homer, there's an
> at once lovely and less-than-lovely
> patterning to the brutality that, even as
> they wield it, is only theirs to borrow
> ('And Love You Too')

'Less-than-lovely', not 'ugly', and yet the euphemism feels more awful than its alternative. Moreover, the description of violence as a 'patterning' (like the design of a wallpaper) contains cruelties that are equally tragic and ironic. 'For the gods in Homer', brutality becomes a show – powerful, moving, but ultimately distant – in a way that it both is and cannot be for the human readers of *The Iliad*. Passages such as these are rich and challenging in ways that go far beyond mystification.

The spell wore off

Ryan Dobran (ed.), *The Collected Letters of Charles Olson and J.H. Prynne* (Uni. of New Mexico Press), $75

Reviewed by LEWIS WYNN

The Beatles were the first to burlesque him. In the 1968 film *Yellow Submarine*, John Lennon asks Jeremy Hillary Boob (PhD) whether he must 'always talk in rhyme?' The clownish cartoon replies 'if I spoke prose you'd all find out, I don't know what I talk about! *Ad hoc, ad loc,* and *quid pro quo*: so little time, so much to know!' Whether he was really based on J.H. Prynne or not, Dr Boob rehearses a complaint that has dogged the poet's reception: there's just *so much* to know. (Mr) Prynne's work is notoriously dense, and its 'difficulty' has been located in a gap between what he knows and his readers don't, between the breadth of allusion occasioned by his poems and the amount of labour requisite for 'getting' them. Specialised or technical vocabulary; a wide array of reference; 'contorted' syntax – the damages are listed and the charge arrives on cue: 'how can a reader be expected to know so much?' It's a gripe that used to hang around Charles Olson, too. In both cases, the apparently innocent question fronts for a demand: *show us only what we know*. But the difficulty of their poetry is really a formal analogue for the belief that alienation won't be overcome by being thematised, no matter how wittily; a resistance to (modern) poets depicting their lot in various shades of pathos, 'only what we know' refracted under the sun of personality – *quid pro quo, ad infinitum*. But engaging with the parody at all can hinder thinking: these heuristics match the poets as equivalent, when their letters show them grow increasingly at odds – even to the point of contradiction.

It wasn't always like this. Prynne opened the correspondence in 1961, asking Olson to publish in *Prospect* – a magazine he edited from Cambridge. He continues by recalling his first encounter with the older poet's work – ('as if reading for the first time the back of my own hand') – and, in response to Olson's published hope for 'a new dictionary of roots', directs him toward Julius Pokorny's *Indogermanisches Etymologisches Wörterbuch*. Olson receives his newest acolyte with open arms – ('the back of our hand for sure') – and encourages Prynne to face 'the derivation problem' head on, a topic that would occupy them both across the following decade. Their shared concern was lyric's emergence from a seeming backdrop of naked desire: how to win song from 'the ambient silences which surround the man on the brink of speech' (Prynne), as well as the role of its 'derived' etymology and syntax. Throughout their exchanges, language is described with the lexis of kinetics – motion, locus, vector – but these forces are given a broad aetiology: whether quantum field theory or Pleistocene coastal morphology, no data is placed outside the problem, and the yield would always find a way back to the poet's breath.

Prynne – then an academic of twenty-four – began spellbound, sending his own poems as an 'emblem of apprenticeship'. This love remains throughout the letters, but the spell wears off. Prynne ended his last letter to Olson – knowingly his last – by casting one of his own: 'from this [letter] you really ought to feel loaned a really haughty stare for anything around you that's boring or obnoxious; because the force of my demand that you be free of such is inalienably magical.' It would be the last time that the young man feigned belief in magic. Prynne had grown apart from Olson by degrees: between providing typescripts for *Maximus Poems IV, V, VI*, teaching Olson's work to his students, and providing his mentor with extensive bibliographies, their earlier sense of shared vocation fades. The scale of their ambition –

encyclopaedically ranging over sources – risked playing fast and loose with information, a risk that Prynne was only willing to take with the due level of care.

In a 1964 exchange, Prynne brings his doubts to the table: wary of Olson's motive for requesting a facsimile on early Greek, he objects that any responsible engagement would require 'more Assyriology', 'more rock': in short, 'all the evidence'. Prynne doesn't speak 'one word of Greek', and to weigh 'the language against its ethical and physical substance, you do need to be very close' – 'or', as he sadly ends, 'I would need it'. 'Lord, Jeremy, I don't know Greek myself', Olson replies, as if Prynne's anxiety was over his *own* shortcomings. Neither poet sought knowledge in order to build up an image-bank for picking themes from, or to feign control over other discourses. Instead, they wished to integrate a broader sample of the world's infinity into the moment of a poem. But for Olson, wishing was commensurate with knowing: the poet would hold the whole world together by sheer force of rhapsody; no lost form of life (or language) was quite lost enough to resist the figure of Maximus. This was too cavalier for Prynne, too lazily omnivorous. Although he shared Olson's desire to expand the permissible limits of musical thinking, he would need to know the Greek – as it were – *before* he spoke it. This conflict over the efficacy of willing was also a question of ethics: Prynne never felt that he could roll the brotherhood of man around his mouth without becoming a cannibal; after all, a wish could never conjure up its own object of knowledge, even less demand its own inalienability.

Prynne and Olson's relationship and correspondence – nearly interchangeable terms, given that the pair only met in person once – show up the whole rubric of 'difficulty' as a soft option, giving the lie to any attempt at equating their intentions. Although the back of Prynne's hand would always look different after meeting Olson's poems, his work proceeds in search of its own distinctive ends, and with its own distinctive methods. Whether or not his poetry becomes any better known (or better read) because of their publication, these letters reveal that the desire to turn Prynne into a surrogate for other discontents is another act of wishful thinking – a dream which draws a caricature no more or less cartoonish than a giddy little drawing on a yellow submarine.

Evacuate the World

Adrienne Rich, *Poetry and Prose*, ed. Albert Gelpi, Barbara Charlesworth Gelpi & Brett C. Millier (Norton), £16.99

Reviewed by IAN POPLE

This is the second Norton Critical Edition of Rich's *Poetry and Prose*; and as such is a teaching edition of Rich's writing. It comprises poetry from Rich's first published volume, *A Change of World*, from 1955, through to her posthumous volume, *Tonight no Poetry will Serve* published in 2013. This book also contains a selection of

Rich's prose published between 1964 and 2005. In addition, there are a range of reviews and criticism, again from a range of commentators from Helen Vendler to Sandra M. Gilbert.

That first collection was chosen by W. H. Auden for the Yale Younger Poets series. His introduction to that book is reprinted here, and in it, he comments that Rich, 'displays a modesty not so common at that age'. Rich was twenty-one when the book was published. That comment on modesty has been pulled out over the years and rather brandished against the later poetry Rich published. The books *Diving into the Wreck* (1973) and *The Dream of a Common Language* were the books that made her name as a feminist intellectual but were dismissed by Elizabeth Hardwick as 'extreme' and 'ridiculous', and Dana Gioia commented at the publication of *Midnight Salvage* in 1999,

'Rich is a major poet overburdened by the role of prophet. She remains an intellectual force, but she has almost vanished as a credible poet, and I for one lament the loss.'

Looking at this volume now, perhaps from the perspective of this side of the Atlantic, and with a certain distance of time, it is the judgement of Dan Chiasson reprinted here, in his review of her *Collected Poems* of 2016, which rings truest. He writes that her 'last books are full of gorgeous evocations of Vermont and California, lonely lyrics that earned their right to evacuate the world and listen to what was left.' It is clear that throughout her writing career, Rich was a close and empathetic observer of that world. Thus her writing, even where it might seem most polemical, was sustained by richness of the real. In her essay on Emily Dickinson, Rich describes driving Dickinson's house in Amherst, and she cannot resist writing, 'cloudy skies breaking into warm sunshine, light-green spring softening the hills, dog-wood and wild fruit-trees blossoming in the hollows,' the kind of precision which occurs in even her most driven, direct writing.

Feeling with the Creatures

Mária Ferenčuhová, *Tidal Events: Selected Poems*, trans. James Sutherland-Smith (Shearsman), £9.95; Luljeta Lleshanaku, *Negative Space*, trans. by Ani Gjika (Bloodaxe), £12

Reviewed by I A N   S E E D

Mária Ferenčuhová was born in Bratislava in 1975. As well as being a poet with four collections to her name, Ferenčuhová is editor of the film magazine *King-Icon*, has written a study of documentary film, and is a translator from French. This is worth mentioning because the aesthetics of both film and French literature evidently inform her poetry. The presence of Baudelaire, for example, can be felt in Ferenčuhová's 'City Map' and 'Illuminated Cities' sequences. As for film, I would venture that there is a neorealist ethics and aesthetics at work. By 'neorealism', one should not understand some kind of heavy socialist realism – far from it – but rather an experimental neorealism in the manner that Italo Calvino practised and theorised in the 1940s. In neorealism, the reality being 're-presented' can be as fragmented as it is cohesive in order to reproduce distortions in perceptions, caused, for example, by the experience of living through a bombing raid or more simply of walking through the streets of a city where what one sees, hears and smells is constantly changing. Ferenčuhová's writing is also neorealist in the sense that it is a committed literature. Just as neorealism emerged from the devastation of World War II, so much of Ferenčuhová's poetry comes out of the destruction of our ecological system.

Her poetry navigates the impact of the way we live, both on us as individual human beings and more widely on our environment. Rather than being visionary in any grandiose sense, it brings reality to life through observations of the minute:

Yellowish cigarette butts
moisten between the blades of grass,
ladybirds, sloe bugs and winged ants
that attack from the back. ('Starfish')

As well as exploring our human perceptions, there is throughout an exhortation for us to consider equally valid ways of experiencing the world by creatures other than ourselves:

mice also quick:
underground. in colour. under seats.
they seek food. between two trains.
utterly deafened: they follow – like you –
trembling wheels legs. ('In the City of Dogs')

After all, there is always a necessary relationship between human beings and the earth. What we abandon will be used by forms of life we don't as a rule spend time thinking about:

The last dead factory.
Masonry has long since given in.
Greenery grows out of it.
Insects have undermined foundations,
surviving in the cracks
and feeding birdlife. ('Starfish')

In Ferenčuhová's sequences, there is a constant search for what we can learn from the forgotten, the strange, the dispossessed. It is from our acknowledgement of these that some kind of real change might come rather than from 'dailyness – passing the days, / working, holding on to life, running to God / only in moments of fear ('The Uncertainty Principle', p. 80). Nevertheless, even in this dailyness, 'grace' may come 'suddenly, from behind your back, / from within like the first movement of a child in your body' (ibid.).

At the heart of this collection is a deeply ecological concern tied in with a quest for existential authenticity, or in religious terms for a vita nova. As translator James Sutherland-Smith points out in his excellent introduction, Ferenčuhová shows that only a sense of individual responsibility and an awareness of our interconnectedness will preserve us from a terrible apathy and despair:

It doesn't take much: touch the earth
like one's own skin,
let the nervous system
overgrow through the border of the body
take root,
descend to the depths of the river,
not to persist in running,
to stop,
give. ('Threatened Species')

Albania's Luljeta Lleshanaku grew up in what she terms the 'negative space' of autocratic communist rule, living under family house arrest during the time when the notorious Enver Hoxha was head of state. Her work has something in common with that of fellow Albanian poet Gëzim Hajdari, whose writing was refused publication in the 1970s because of its emphasis on the interior life of the individual. The poetry in *Negative Space* is Lleshanaku's response to what was not only absent from her own life but also from that of an entire generation.

It is the accumulation of specific, concrete detail in these poems which makes the places and the people that inhabit them truly individual, one might say truly restored to themselves after decades of denial. Childhood memory navigated through sensory imagery is the key to unlocking the past, as in this excerpt from a portrait of a one-armed history teacher, who in the end cannot stop himself from unwittingly subverting his recitation of facts with his own humanity, for, 'while we could hardly wait for the bell / to write our own history':

> sometimes his hollow sleeve
> felt warm and human, like a cricket-filled summer night.
> It hovered, waiting to land somewhere. On a valley or roof.
> It searched for a hero among us –
> not among the athletic or sparkly-eyed ones,
> but among those stamped with innocence. ('History Class')

In these memories a child's perspective is often contrasted with that of an adult, who will naturally have far more material concerns in the struggle for survival, for example in this story of a doll, 'one of the few things my mother saved':

> It was the same height as my six-year old self,
> with the same grey-coloured eyes, brown hair,
> the same fear of the dark
> and drawn to it.
> 'Don't touch her!' I was told.
> 'I have nothing else to sell if we go broke!'

> Until the day I secretly stole her
> and broke her heel by accident.
> It was worth nothing now. No capital.
> And then it became mine. ('Mine, Yours')

Sometimes the memories take the form of vignettes, seemingly comic and throwaway, yet powerfully poignant, as in the series of one-line portraits of women in 'Commit to Memory', including:

> P. who got along well with her mother-in-law.
> S. who had an abortion every six months.
> T. with a sweet laugh and always a run on her stockings.
> N. who roasted good coffee when she had any.
> R. who secretly used to sell her own blood.
> Z. who picked up her son's guts with her own hands
> the day he was hit by a freight train.

Lleshanaku also has a much wider sense of time and place which goes beyond her own memories to encompass other eras and continents. In the poem just quoted she compares her memories of the women she's known to the inscription on the gravestone of a Roman woman from 135 BC. Histories intertwine. The long poem 'Homo Antarcticus' tracks the fate of an explorer who could adapt to months of near-starvation in sub-zero Antarctica but not to later life back in normal society. It is the tension between individual desires and societal pressures which makes this collection such a compelling one.

The poetry from Central and Eastern Europe which came in the aftermath of World War II and the Holocaust is regarded by some as the best poetry to be written in the latter half of the twentieth century – see, for example, *The Poetry of Survival: Poet-War Poets of Central and Eastern Europe*, edited by Daniel Weissbort (Penguin, 1993). The collections reviewed here are proof that poetry from this part of the world is still powerful and affecting.

— COLOPHON —

Editors
Michael Schmidt (General)
Andrew Latimer (Deputy)

Editorial address
The Editors at the address on the right. Manuscripts cannot be returned unless accompanied by a stamped addressed envelope or international reply coupon.

Trade distributors
NBN International
10 Thornbury Road
Plymouth PL6 7PP, UK
orders@nbninternational.com

Design
Luke Allan
Typeset by Andrew Latimer
  in Arnhem Pro.

Represented by
Compass IPS Ltd
Great West House
Great West Road, Brentford
TW8 9DF, UK
sales@compass-ips.london

Copyright
© 2018 Poetry Nation Review
All rights reserved
ISBN 978-1-78410-155-8
ISSN 0144-7076

Subscriptions (6 issues)
INDIVIDUALS (print and digital): £39.50; abroad £49
INSTITUTIONS (print only): £76; abroad £90
INSTITUTIONS (digital): subscriptions from Exact Editions (https://shop.exacteditions.com/gb/pn-review)
to: *PN Review*, Alliance House, 30 Cross Street, Manchester M2 7AQ, UK

Supported by